EDISON JONES AND THE ANTI-GRAV ELEVATOR

MICHAEL SCOTT CLIFTON

BOOKS BY
MICHAEL SCOTT CLIFTON

The Treasure Hunt Club

The Janus Witch

Conquest of the Veil Series

The Open Portal

(Coming Spring 2020)

Escape From Wheel

Edison Jones Series

Edison Jones and The Anti-Grav Elevator

Book Liftoff
1209 South Main Street
PMB 126
Lindale, Texas 75771

This book is a work of fiction. Therefore, all names, places, characters, and situations are a product of the author's imagination and used fictitiously. Any resemblance to actual persons, living or dead, places, or events is entirely coincidental.
Copyright © 2020 Michael Scott Clifton

Interior's book design by Champagne Book Design
champagnebookdesign.com

Clifton, Michael Scott
Edison Jones and The Anti-Grav Elevator / Michael Scott Clifton
1. Action & Adventure / Literature & Fiction / Teen & Young Adult
2. Boys & Men / Literature & Fiction / Teen & Young Adult.
3. Fiction / Teen & Young Adult
BISAC: YAF000000 YOUNG ADULT FICTION / General
YAF001000 YOUNG ADULT FICTION / Action & Adventure / General
YAF007000 YOUNG ADULT FICTION / Boys & Men
YAF058150 YOUNG ADULT FICTION / Social Themes / New Experiences
YAF058110 YOUNG ADULT FICTION / Social Themes / Friendship

ISBN: 978-1-947946-52-1

www.michaelscottclifton.com
www.bookliftoff.com

To all public and private educators. May you continue to inspire wonder and curiosity in your students.

"What a man's mind can create, man's character can control"
—Thomas Edison

EDISON JONES AND THE ANTI-GRAV ELEVATOR

CHAPTER 1

THE DRONE DROPPED FROM THE SKY.

It hovered silently above the smashed and broken car, recording the scene. Steam fumed in a geyser from the crumpled radiator, a rain of shattered safety glass making a *rat-a-tat* tinkling sound. A metallic groan came from the frame of the heavy SUV as it settled onto a puckered roof. The *hiss* of steam slowly petered out, and the pieces of glass stopped falling.

Nothing moved.

A book lay on the ground next to the crumpled Escalade. Pages with pictures of dinosaurs fluttered in the breeze. A sound like a clock slowly winding down came from the crushed engine.

Tick…tick….tick…..tick.

And then…silence.

The drone rose and disappeared.

CHAPTER 2

(Seven Years Later)

At the *ping*, twelve-year old Edison Jones smiled in satisfaction.

He reached down and uncoupled the power cable from his wheelchair and toggled a joystick. With a soft *whirr*, the wheels folded up and disappeared under the seat. Rather than sinking to the floor, however, the chair bobbed a few times before settling into a hover position a few feet above the ground.

"Yes!" Edison shouted and pumped his fist into the air.

His former wheelchair now acted as though weightless, and he eagerly manipulated the controls on the arm of the hoverchair. It rose higher, then lower, before spinning in a 360-degree rotation. Edison pushed a joystick forward, and shot around his bedroom, looping up and over his bed, table, and other furniture like a roller-coaster ride. The lamp stand beside his bed suddenly appeared, and rather than going over or around, Edison decided to try something different and engaged the controls in full reverse.

His anti-grav chair stopped on a dime!

"Awesome!" Edison whooped. His elation quickly deflated at the reality of what this day represented.

The start of his first day—*ever*—in a public school.

From the age of five, his education was handled by a succession of private tutors. This left him with abundant time to pursue his passion for inventions and technological development. His voracious curiosity knew no limits, matched only by his willingness to push each of his projects to the absolute threshold of possibility.

He loved every minute of it…and now his grandpa insisted he attend a public school.

With a heavy sigh, he rotated the hoverchair to face the east wall of his bedroom. "Enable," he commanded.

The entire wall went opaque temporarily before resolving into an undersea scene with three dimensional clarity. A colorful reef presented itself. Yellow parrotfish darted in and out of the swaying tentacles of sea anemones. A giant, green sea turtle paddled by a bulging growth of reddish brain coral. Another scene appeared, this one of a snow-covered alpine vista with towering firs thrusting upward toward the clear, blue sky. Reluctantly, Edison turned away and tapped a key on the hoverchair's control console. The pleasant panorama disappeared, and the wall resolved into a giant mirror.

A thin boy with deep-set green eyes, stared back at Edison. He ran fingers through his thatch of curly, brown hair in a fruitless attempt to tame the unruly mane. Lips pursed in concentration, he studied the light scattering of freckles on his pale complexion. For some reason their configuration always reminded him of the Andromeda constellation.

If I could stand, I would be tall for my age.

Edison shook his head. *But since I can't stand, and won't ever be able to stand, its illogical to even think about it.* Frustrated, he barked, "Terminate!" The mirror disappeared to become his bedroom wall once again.

Edison balled his hands into fists. *Why can't Grandpa understand? I don't want to go to school here or anyplace else.*

I want to be left alone, just like always.

"We need to go, Edison," Stanton Jones called from the bottom of the stairs. "You don't want to be late on your first day of school."

Although almost seventy-years old, Stanton Jones wore an erect bearing, his close-cropped hair and goatee dark with only a few wisps of grey salted through it. Sparkling blue eyes belied an intellectual intensity and insatiable curiosity that had allowed Jones to build a startup company, LogicTech, in his garage some forty years earlier, then develop it into one of the world's largest technology firms.

Jones had no doubt what his grandson was engaged in at that very moment—tinkering with his latest invention—confirmation Edison inherited the same intense curiosity.

Edison's voice drifted down. "I'll be finished in just a sec, Grandpa."

"Very well. Be quick about it, though," Jones warned. "We're downstairs waiting."

"Is he coming?" a concerned voice asked from behind Jones. He turned and nodded at a powerfully built man.

Carney Caruso shook his head. An ex-navy SEAL, he doubled as Edison's bodyguard and physical therapist. Polar blue eyes looked out from below dark, brown hair buzz-cut so severe, that the flat plane resembled a carrier deck. Hard muscles rippled underneath Carney's polo shirt and slacks as he paced back and forth.

Jones patted Carney on the shoulder. "He'll be along shortly."

Carney wore a doubtful expression. "I don't know, sir. He's not looking forward to this."

The LogicTech CEO frowned at the sight of the bodyguard's worried expression. He had no wish to revisit the same discussion they had argued about countless times. They both knew why Edison dreaded the arrival of the first day of school. His private tutors allowed him to stay immersed in his inventions, while the car wreck which robbed him of the use of his legs also left him extremely sensitive to his paraplegia.

Edison wanted no one to point out or otherwise emphasize his paralysis.

Grief clouded Jones' eyes. Images of the mangled SUV and the black body bags containing his son and daughter-in-law flashed through his mind. And then a final picture...Edison's small, blood-covered body being rushed to the hospital on that horrific day seven years ago.

Other memories surfaced, and Jones clenched his teeth. Independent of the police, he directed an alternate investigation into the accident. This revealed proof the computer chip controlling the Escalade's electronic system was replaced with another—then slaved wirelessly to a master controller. The inquiry led to an inescapable conclusion.

The accident was a deliberate act of cold-blooded murder.

If not for a last second emergency at LogicTech's Austin, Texas fabrication plant, Jones would have been in the vehicle as well. *He* was the intended target, his family collateral damage.

Jones dug fingernails into the soft flesh of his palms to force his thoughts back to the present.

"He's twelve-years old, Carney," Jones managed to say, thus sparking their old debate, "and he's been stuck in *this* house and *that* wheelchair since he was five. It's time he got out into the real world to meet boys and girls his own age. He can't stay shut away from society and life forever."

"But he's happy, sir!" Carney protested. "Edison assists you in the lab, he invents new devices all the time...and his education hasn't suffered. How many kids his age are taking an online college algebra course for heaven's sake? How can a public school top that?"

Jones dismissed the comment with a weary wave of his hand. "You miss the point. I don't want my grandson to grow up like some hermit in a cave, totally shut off from society. That can't be healthy. It isn't healthy!"

"What about Edison's paralysis? You know he's sensitive, and the first time some kid points at his wheelchair—"

"I am well aware of the possibility!" Jones barked. A tense moment passed between the two men before Jones's expression softened.

"Look, Carney, I understand your concern. But when you say Edison is happy, I couldn't disagree more. Happiness defined as what? The only friends he has are his computers, the inventions he tinkers with, the staff, and you and me. He knows not one, not a *single* person his age! That's not happiness, Carney, it's solitary confinement, and God forgive me, it's a prison I've helped create for him." Unshed tears shone from Jones's eyes.

Carney reached out and placed a hand on Jones's shoulder. "I know you love Edison, sir. I-I didn't mean to imply otherwise."

A chuckle slipped from the normally stoic Jones, and he wiped his eyes with the back of his hand. "Well, I think that makes two of us, Carney, because you have been as much a father to him as if he were your own."

Jones gazed up the stairs. "You're right about Edison's disability. Sooner or later, someone will give him an odd look or say something about it. But at some point he's going to have to deal with it." With a sigh of resignation, Jones turned and looked at Carney.

"It's a cross he'll bear the rest of his life."

CHAPTER 3

With a flick of his wrist, Edison's chair floated from the room. Rather than use the motorized platform to carry him down the stairs, Edison nudged the anti-grav chair toward the first step.

Stanton Jones and Carney waited at the foot of the staircase. At the sight of Edison's hoverchair perched precariously on the edge of the stairway, their eyes grew wide. "Edison, stop!" they cried in unison.

Before either Carney or his grandfather could react, Edison grinned and pushed the joystick all the way forward. The wheelchair shot down the staircase and came to a smooth stop at the bottom.

Mouths agape, Jones and Carney stared at Edison. Jones managed to stammer, "Wha-what do you think you're doing? You could have killed yourself!" Carney nodded in vigorous agreement.

Edison laughed. "Relax, Grandpa. I already tested the AGMAG. It works fine."

"The AGMAG? What the hell is that?" Carney demanded.

Edison pointed to a donut-shaped bulge circling the base of his hover chair. "My AGMAG, the anti-gravity magnet I've been working on."

At Carney's look of irate incomprehension, Edison patiently explained, "The AGMAG works on the principal of pushing against the Earth's natural magnetic field. So, I installed an electromagnet in my wheelchair which reverses the magnetic polarity. This creates an anti-gravity field and causes the wheelchair to hover."

Warming to the subject, Edison leaned forward. "A series of smaller electromagnets act like gyros. They stabilize and cause my anti-grav chair to change direction. That was the easy part. The hard part was creating a hydrogen fuel cell with enough storage capacity to charge the electromagnets, and still last a reasonable amount of time."

Edison shrugged. "I still have some bugs to work out, but with normal usage, my calculations indicate the current fuel cell should last at least forty-eight hours."

Carney looked at Jones and shook his head. "You may know what he is talking about, sir, but he might as well be talking Greek to me."

Stanton Jones clapped the ex-SEAL on the back. "It means *it's time for us to go to school.*"

Edison sat in the backseat, the countryside passing by in a blur as they crossed the I-30 corridor between Texarkana and Dallas. According to GPS, the trip from the Jones Mansion to Harpersville Junior High School should take less than fifteen minutes. He tracked their progress on the tablet he held in his lap, his apprehension rising the nearer they drew to the school.

The black Mercedes joined a score of cars lined up in front of the junior high with parents dropping off their children. Excited throngs of chattering students stood about the horseshoe-shaped area lined with trees and concrete benches.

Edison gulped. *I've never seen so many kids.*

Carney brought the sedan to a stop before popping the trunk latch to retrieve Edison's wheelchair. The ex-SEAL exited the car...then stopped short.

The chair hovered above the trunk.

The anti-grav chair unfolded. The seat back swiveled up and snapped into place. With a soft *whir*, the armrests rose from a recessed position. Last, the footrests telescoped out from the frame. Floating two feet off the ground, the chair moved silently around the corner of the car and came to a stop beside Edison's open door. Grinning at the look on Carney's face, Edison transferred from the car into the seat.

Edison settled in and asked, "Can you hand me my backpack, Grandpa?"

Chuckling, Jones handed Edison his knapsack before he too, exited the sedan.

"Remote control," Edison quipped in response to the incredulous look still on Carney's face. He pointed to a slim, watch-sized data device strapped to his wrist. "I've designed the anti-grav chair so the frame acts like a wireless antenna and receiver. The same technology has been used in cell phones for years. Simple, really."

Carney shook his head. "Oh. Right."

Edison floated forward a foot above the ground. The sight of the hoverchair soon caught the notice of the crowd gathered at the entrance. Edison's face flushed when some of the students pointed at him while their parents whispered furiously to one another. He gritted his teeth.

The moment of truth had arrived.

Stanton Jones put a hand on Edison's shoulder. "Want me to go with you?"

Edison hung his backpack on the back of the hoverchair, and sat up straight. Light from the morning sun glinted off the row of glass doors. "No. I have to do this myself, Grandpa."

Edison turned. "And I know why you want me to do this. I hope I don't disappoint you."

With a deep breath, he propelled his anti-grav chair forward.

Stanton Jones followed Edison's progress. He noted the reaction the sight his grandson stirred among the students and parents. For the hundredth time, he hoped he had made the right decision.

A lump rose in his throat as Edison stopped at the entrance and turned to give them a final wave. Jones waved back as his grandson propelled through an open door.

And disappeared from sight.

CHAPTER 4

Edison stopped inside the foyer to consult the class schedule he pulled from his backpack. Although he had already visited Harpersville ISD's website to take the virtual tour of the facilities, he still needed to get his bearings.

While he studied his schedule, a shadow fell over him. "Do you need some help?"

A girl about his age stood peering at him over a pair of wire-frame glasses. Olive-skinned with shoulder-length black hair, she clutched a class schedule of her own.

A surge of anger coursed through Edison. *Here we go. The first example of someone who thinks I'm helpless.* He opened his mouth to provide a quick retort, but the girl smiled to reveal braces, her brown eyes glowing warmly.

Edison's mouth snapped shut.

The girl adjusted her folders and class schedule to her left hand then held out her right. "I'm Briana Mata but just call me Bree. Everybody does."

Edison gulped and stared for a moment or two. Slowly, he reached out and gripped Bree's outstretched hand. It was warm and smooth to the touch.

"Pl-pleased to meet you, Bree," he stuttered.

Bree released Edison's hand and held out her own.

"May I?" she asked.

Again, Edison stared, confused, before he finally realized what she wanted. He passed her his schedule.

Bree scanned it and smiled. "We have three classes together including first period science." Seconds later the bell rang signaling the start of school. Students poured in through the open doors, jostling both of them like driftwood in an incoming tide.

"C'mon, we can go to first period together!" she shouted over the noise. Motioning for him to follow, she navigated her way through the densely packed hallway.

Edison manipulated the controls to trail his new friend. More than a few stares and pointing fingers accompanied his progress, but Edison was curiously immune to all of it. He had dreaded his first day of school and didn't really know what to expect. He never anticipated what just happened.

That he would make a friend within his first five minutes there.

After a short trip around a hallway corner, Edison and Bree arrived at their science class. Along the way, Bree greeted several of her friends, always taking care to introduce Edison to each of them. Time didn't allow for uncomfortable silence after every introduction with each student in a hurry to get to their classes. Bree swept Edison along with her and kept him busy negotiating through the heavy student traffic.

They burst through the open doorway of a classroom. Bree chose a desk near the front and threw her backpack on top of it, then removed the chair from the desk next to hers. She waved at Edison, and he maneuvered his hoverchair into the space. The desks were actually tables, and his hoverchair slid easily into the area beneath it. He settled in, and looked over at his new friend. A glint of curiosity sparked in her eyes.

She pointed. "How does it move? I don't see any wheels."

"Yeah, dude, what's up with that?" a voice asked from behind Bree. A large boy sprawled forward on a desk, his lantern-like chin resting on muscular arms. Thick, sandy brown hair sprouted in an untidy mass from his head, and a pair of sleepy, blue eyes stared curiously at Edison. A sun-darkened tan painted his cheeks and nose, and with a huge yawn, he pointed again.

"I mean, are you like Secret Agent 007 or something?"

Edison's cheeks burned. He opened his mouth but before he could respond, Bree blurted, "Hondo, that's rude! It's Edison's first day."

"No offense, dude. Just wonderin', that's all. Name's Hondo Edwards by the way." Still sprawled, he stretched a large, closed fist forward.

Edison blinked and recoiled. After a moment's hesitation, Bree took his hand, firmly closed it in a fist, and bumped it against Hondo's. *Oh. Another form of greeting.* Sheepish, his confusion ebbed away.

Before he could retrieve his hand, a girl hurtled through the open door of the classroom seconds ahead of the tardy bell.

Bree rolled her eyes. "Carly, late as usual."

Taking the student table in front of Edison, Carly tossed her backpack to the ground and pivoted.

"Can you believe we are already having cheer practice? The first football game's a month away, so what's the rush? Did you see what Madison Wilcox is wearing? *Hello!* Doesn't she realize wearing Ugg boots with shorts is a fashion disgrace? And OMG, did you see the outfit on sale at *Allie's Boutique* in the mall? Can you believe my mother wouldn't let me get it because she said it was too 'mature' for me? When I argued with her, she threatened to take my phone away *and* cancel my texting privileges! I mean, life would end, I might as well be dead, and oh, hi, Hondo." Carly batted her eyes at the large boy.

Edison gaped. *How could anyone talk so fast?* The words gushed from Carly's mouth in an unbroken rush like an uncapped oil well. Convinced she hadn't paused to take a single breath during her entire conversation, he belatedly noticed how pretty she was. Blonde hair cascaded down her back like a golden waterfall, and clear blue eyes perched above a pert nose. Full lips covered perfect rows of white teeth, while Carly's cream-colored skin framed an unblemished, heart-shaped face.

She is the most beautiful girl I've ever seen.

Captivated, Edison didn't realize for a moment the teacher was talking until Bree, a peevish look on her face, reached over and rapped the arm of the hoverchair.

Embarrassed, he returned his attention to the class, where their science teacher, Mr. Russell, a tall, middle-aged man with graying hair, stood. "Now class, since this is an honors course, you should have already started work on your group project."

A chorus of moans greeted this announcement.

"Speaking of honors, I'm surprised to see you in my class, Hondo," the science teacher said.

Hondo spread his arms. "I know, right? The counselor said this science class was the only one which would fit my schedule. Believe me, I tried to get the regular science class."

Laughter rocked the room, and Mr. Russell quickly raised his hand. "Since we will begin with the study of cells, you will not only construct both a plant and an animal cell model, but provide a digital presentation to the class as well." Another round of moans commenced which Mr. Russell ignored. He looked at Edison, then glanced at the class roster. *"Edison Jones.* I see you registered late this summer. Did you have a chance to look at the syllabus and begin work on your cell project?"

Edison froze at the unexpected attention of the two dozen faces directed toward him. Comfortable and at ease amongst LogicTech engineers and researchers, Edison found the scrutiny of his fellow seventh-graders unnerving. He gulped and tried to speak several times. Finally, he pressed the screen on the slim data device strapped to his wrist..

A holographic, three dimensional image of a plant cell leaped into the air above the tiny computer. *Oohs* and *aahs* filled the room. This increased in intensity as Edison manipulated the touchscreen and caused the cell image to rotate in midair.

Emboldened by the class's favorable reaction, Edison managed to state, "I thought I would begin by creating a 3-D image of plant and animal cells. Then I wrote a program which adds cell organelles, highlights them, and labels them." He made another adjustment, and within the cell, the nucleus, and other organelles appeared in bright colors of blue, green, and red. Each organelle's name blinked beside it in a neon-bright light.

Mr. Russell gaped with the same fascination as his students. He managed to say, "Uh, that's great, Edison. It looks like you have things under control."

The science teacher turned back to the class. "Since Edison is a new student, he hasn't been assigned to a group. Would anybody like to volunteer to be part of Edison's team?"

A long pause followed and the students in class looked at each other. Edison's face flushed, and he wished he could teleport himself a million miles away. Then, moments later, hands shot up and chaos exploded.

"I'll be on Edison's team!" one girl shouted.

"Hey, I had my hand up first!" a boy next to her cried.

Students from all over the classroom shouted to be heard. This went on for several moments as Mr. Russell unsuccessfully tried to regain control of the class. Then a loud voice from behind Edison sliced through the clamor. *"I'll be in his group!"*

Edison glanced over his shoulder. Hondo stood, the sleepy appearance gone, a determined look on his face. Immediately, the verbal tumult subsided. No student spoke up to challenge the large boy's claim.

Mr. Russell cleared his throat and managed to say, "Thank you, Hondo. Okay, we have one student on Edison's team, we need two more."

Carly, who followed Hondo's exchange keenly, raised her hand and stood. "I think Edison ought to be able to choose the rest of the members of his group, Mr. Russell." She moved around her table, and with a smile, put her hand on Edison's shoulder. "I know I would *love* to be a member of your team."

Tongue-tied, Edison barely registered Mr. Russell's agreement with Carly. With great effort, he managed to stammer, "Ca-Carly will be fine with me." He slumped in relief then spied Bree, her lips pressed into a weak smile.

Quickly, he blurted, "And Bree! I'd like Bree to be in my group too!" Her eyes lit up and she clapped with delight.

Although grumbling continued from students who hadn't been picked, it seemed to settle the matter, and Mr. Russell went through the remainder of the class syllabus without further incident.

The rest of the day went by in a blur.

Edison went to each of his classes and met his new teachers and classmates. He discovered Carly—along with Bree—also shared some of his classes, although his only common period with Hondo was science. The curious looks and whispers he received—so numerous when he first hovered through the school doors—disappeared by the end of the day. His fellow students viewed him no differently than those who walked the hallways on two legs. His fear and uncertainty melted away to be replaced with a warm sense of acceptance.

He liked the feeling. He liked his new friends.

And he liked his first day ever in a public school.

Stanton Jones had just concluded a Skype conference with a LogicTech plant manager in Thailand when he heard the front door slam. He stood, stretched, and tapped a key. The monitor disappeared through a slotted recess in the desk, and he walked out of his office. He rubbed tired eyes and cursed the fact an emergency at the plant caused him to miss picking Edison up from school with Carney. He quickly made his way to the door. As he stepped into the foyer, he almost collided with Edison's anti-grav chair.

"Grandpa! I made three friends at school today and we're going to work on a science project together. The whole class wanted to be in my group, and I got to pick who I wanted! Anyway, I have a few more ideas for the project and I'm going to go work on them!"

Within seconds of the words tumbling from his mouth, Edison turned and rocketed the hoverchair up the stairs. Astonished, Jones turned to Carney who wore an ear-to-ear grin.

"It's all he talked about the entire ride home…the friends he met, the project they're going to work on—and how he can't *wait* for school tomorrow."

Carney walked to the foot of the stairs. He gazed upward for a few moments before he glanced back at Jones.

The battle-hardened ex-SEAL's eyes were moist. "Five years ago, you hired me when Edison was only seven, and I can tell you without a doubt, I have never seen him happier than today."

You were right, sir. You were right all along."

CHAPTER 5

Edison looked up at the clatter of a lunch tray next to him in the cafeteria.

Hondo fell into a chair. "Whatcha doing?"

Edison held up a wafer-thin tablet. "Just reviewing notes from my third period Texas History class."

The sour expression on Hondo's face indicated what he thought of *that*.

Edison smiled at the challenges he had faced since enrolling in school several weeks earlier. His accelerated honors courses were not a problem. Instead, his learning curve turned out to be interpreting social interactions. The ebb and flow of life as a twelve-year-old in junior high proved more daunting than he ever imagined.

And very much a work in progress.

Moments later, Bree joined them. She opened a book and read silently while she ate a sandwich. Edison, disappointed Carly wasn't with her, spotted the cheerleader in the far corner of the cafeteria surrounded by a group of friends. She moved with ease from one cluster of students to another. He tracked her blonde head bobbing like a cork as she worked her way across the crowded lunchroom. As usual, her mouth was in constant motion.

"Edison, since you're a brainiac," Hondo drawled through a mouthful of food, "how 'bout helping me in some of my classes? Coach said I got three failing notices on my progress report."

Hondo's unexpected request wrenched Edison's attention away from Carly. At a momentary loss of words, Bree spared him an immediate answer when she interjected, "Hondo, you *never* study! That's why you have trouble passing."

Hondo shrugged. "Can't see how knowing something 'bout a dude's been dead for a hundred years, or how to conjugate a verb is ever going to help me in life. Besides, someday I'm going to be an NFL quarterback, and I'll *pay* somebody to tell me that stuff!"

Bree flipped her eyes. "You're hopeless."

"So, whatcha think, Edison?" Hondo persisted. "Can you help me? I can't play in the first game next week unless I bring my grades up."

"Uh, sure, Hondo," Edison replied. "Did you want me to come over to your house after school?"

"No!" Hondo replied sharply. "My old lady works nights and she'll be asleep. Can't you just pick me up after practice?" Bree looked up, then quickly averted her eyes back to her book.

Edison blinked, taken aback by Hondo's outburst. Finally, he managed to say, "Sure. I'll get Carney to pick us up after football practice today. We can study at, uh, my house." The big boy nodded stiffly then got up and dumped his tray in a nearby trash can. Moments later, he stalked out of the cafeteria.

"What did I say?" Edison asked.

Bree, lips pursed, watched Hondo's retreating back. She turned back to face Edison. "Hondo doesn't get along with his mother's boyfriend. His home life is...complicated. I don't know a lot about it, except he doesn't like to go home much. Last year, he came to school with a black eye. He said he was playing baseball and missed the ball. But everybody thinks he got into a fight with the boyfriend."

"What happened to his father?" At the look on Bree's face, Edison immediately regretted the question.

"He doesn't have a father! Don't you get it, Edison?" Bree snapped. "Look, you're the smartest person in the entire seventh grade, maybe the smartest person I have ever met, but you have a lot to learn about life and the way things are!" With that, Bree snapped her book shut, got up, and walked away.

Stunned, Edison watched her leave and tried to process what just happened. He put his tablet down with a sigh. Bree was right.

He *did* have a lot to learn.

Edison arrived early for football practice after school. The practice field was located adjacent to the larger junior high football stadium. The seventh-grade team, in red jerseys, toiled on the smaller practice field while the eighth grade team, in blue jerseys, practiced in the football stadium. Earlier, he texted Carney and his grandfather to let them know where he would be and when to pick him up. He maneuvered his hoverchair to get the best possible vantage point, then settled in on the sideline to watch.

Edison's scant knowledge of football was due to the fact he spent much of his time tinkering with projects, giving him little time for anything else. However, he could tell after only five minutes of observation that Hondo was *very* good at it. His large friend stood a head taller than most of the other members of the seventh-grade team. Despite his size, Hondo, with the yellow quarterback jersey on, proved quick and mobile enough to easily elude the rush of the defensive linemen. On consecutive plays, he lofted a pass at least forty yards downfield with pinpoint accuracy into the arms of a receiver, then on the very next play, he ran the ball into the end zone dragging three would-be tacklers with him.

A pang of envy coursed through Edison as he watched Hondo's impressive physical talents. *What would it be like to run like him? To race like the wind in front of a stadium full of cheering fans?* He shook his head, angry at such thoughts. He couldn't even stand much less run!

To occupy his time and attention on something else, he rummaged around in his backpack and removed what appeared to be a thick black pen. He inserted the "pen" into a circular port recessed into the arm of his anti-grav chair so it pointed straight into the air like a flagpole. Next, he telescoped the cylindrical object upward to more or less eye-level and removed a cap which covered its tip. This revealed a small camera lens, and a tiny red LED light pulsed on and off behind the lens. He removed his tablet from the backpack, powered it up, and synced it with the pen, a miniaturized digital video camera. Moments later, Hondo's image appeared on the tablet's screen. Manipulating the controls on the hoverchair's arm, Edison zoomed in on the football practice. Satisfied, he enabled the camera's motion detector function to follow and record the players' movements.

An hour and a half later, practice finished, Hondo walked toward Edison while he briskly tapped away on his tablet's touch screen.

Hondo stopped a short distance away. "Here, catch!" Football in one large hand, he tossed it.

Startled, Edison dropped the digital device, brought his hands up, and nimbly caught the football. Shocked, he gawked at it.

Hondo grinned. "Nice catch! You have better hands than our receivers!"

"Huh? Oh, yeah, thanks," Edison sputtered.

He recovered quickly and held the tablet's screen so Hondo could see it. "Look at this." Video from the mini-cam rolled across the monitor.

Edison fast forwarded through parts of the digital footage. "I did a statistical analysis of the practice and discovered when you run the ball on the left side of the line, you average five-point-six yards more per carry. However, when you pass the ball on the right side of the field, you average ten-point-three yards per pass."

Hondo stared, his mouth agape. Finally, he said, "Lemme see the video again!"

"Sure." Edison scrolled through the footage while Hondo had him stop and start at certain points.

Hondo whistled. "You gotta show this to Coach Macklin! He runs the offense in practice." Hondo turned and ran back to the fieldhouse and returned moments later with one of the seventh-grade coaches.

A large, beefy man, Leonard Macklin stood at just over six feet tall, with a neck that started and ended at his shoulders. With excited gestures, Hondo had Edison show Coach Macklin the film of the practice and the statistical analysis he made. After the demonstration, Macklin took a step back, eyebrows raised.

"And you don't even *watch* football on TV?" he asked in disbelief.

Edison, a crooked grin on his face, shook his head. "But whether or not I watch football, the physical laws governing force, mass, and motion are the same. I applied these laws to football, and it was a simple matter of making a statistical model which fit within the game's parameters."

Speechless, Coach Macklin gaped. Hondo clapped him on the back and cheerfully said, "It's okay, Coach. Edison talks like that all the time. He kinda can't help himself."

Macklin shook his head as if to clear away the grogginess of a deep slumber, then said, "Well, I have just one question for you, Edison."

"Yes, Coach?"

"You want to be our statistician?"

CHAPTER 6

On the way home, Edison listened to Carney and Hondo engage in a spirited discussion of football lasting until they reached the outskirts of town. Hondo excitedly recounted Edison's video analysis of the practice, and how Coach Macklin asked him to be the team's statistician.

Listening to the pleasant banter, Edison was struck by how eager Hondo seemed when he talked to Carney. *Did it have anything to do with having no father? The abusive boyfriend? Maybe he just didn't have anyone to talk to?* His head ached to think about it, and as they turned onto the road leading to the Jones Mansion, he came to a conclusion.

Life might be the hardest problem of all to decipher.

A white rail fence announced the boundaries of the Jones property. Meticulously maintained, the railing ran parallel with the road for almost a mile before Carney turned onto their private, asphalt lane with a locked metal gate. The ex-SEAL pressed a button on the console of the Mercedes. A black, wrought-iron gate with a large "J" positioned in the middle, rolled open. Live oaks lined either side of the lane, and after driving several hundred yards, a large, two-story mansion appeared. Water sprayed from a bronze nymph in a large, aquatic garden as they pulled into a spacious, six-car garage.

Hondo's jaw dropped. "This is your house?"

"Yes," Edison replied.

"Your family must be rich!"

"Rich? Well…I really never thought about it." Lips pursed, Edison added, "The last company earnings report I saw showed a quarterly profit of over ten billion dollars."

"Ten *billion*?" Hondo gasped.

"Yes, I believe that's right. However, that's before taxes and depreciation. Then a lot goes right back into research and devel—"

A loud snort interrupted Edison. He turned to see Carney trying to stifle a laugh at Hondo's incredulous reaction to Edison's accountant-like answer. The ex-SEAL stumbled from the vehicle and managed to mumble, "See you guys later." He sprinted toward a nearby door, laughter spilling from his lips.

Peeved, Edison decided his learning curve just got tossed another juicy softball. It never occurred to him to consider the difference in lifestyle between the rich and everyone else. From the look on Hondo's face, it must be a big one indeed.

Determined not to appear any more foolish than he already felt, Edison directed his hoverchair from the trunk next to the backseat. He quickly slid into the seat and made a beeline for the same opening Carney disappeared through. He waited as Hondo took a last look around, then followed behind his friend.

They moved forward and the door swung silently open. Hondo studied the door, its smooth surface unmarred by any knob or latch. He shook his head. "Guess you don't need a door handle, huh?"

Edison explained, "All entries and exits in the estate are fitted with proximity sensors which scan and recognize biorhythms—mine included. They open and shut doors automatically. The security system won't allow entry for any unauthorized personnel."

Hondo scratched his head. "Personnel?"

Edison's face flushed. "I mean Grandpa, Carney, and trusted household staff. You know—family!"

His big friend grinned. "Just messin' with you, dude."

"Oh, right." Relieved, Edison went into the mansion.

Edison led them deeper into the large manor, his friend's head on a swivel at the sight of the mansion's opulent interior. When they passed the kitchen, Hondo stopped and pointed. "This kitchen is as big as the doublewide I live in!"

They moved into the main foyer. A huge crystal chandelier hung from the ceiling, and cast a warm glow on the polished marble floor. They stopped at the base of a large, winding staircase, the burnished wooden steps gleaming in the light.

Without hesitation, Edison propelled his anti-grav chair up the stairs. It shot up and over the steps with barely a ripple. He stopped at the top, turned, and grinned.

"What are you waiting for?"

"I gotta get me one of those things!" Hondo sprinted upward taking two steps at a time. Laughing, Edison spun the hoverchair and headed for his room with Hondo in hot pursuit.

Edison burst through the open doorway to his bedroom, his friend only a step behind. A ghostly 3-D image of a keyboard appeared and hovered before him. His fingers manipulated spectral keys, and the recessed lights in the ceiling brightened.

"Watch this," Edison said.

All four walls went opaque and then clarified into a desert scene complete with sand dunes stretching into the horizon. A caravan of camels and burnoose-clad riders appeared and plodded past the two boys. Strung out like pearls on a necklace, their silhouettes provided a sharp contrast to the reddish sun behind them. The whisper of blowing sand and grunting camels rang out.

"Awesome!" Hondo shouted.

Edison chuckled. "I thought you'd like it."

"Well, you got that right." He pointed at the desert panorama. "It's like I can reach out and grab a handful of sand. How did you do it?"

Edison shrugged. "Comes natural I guess." His expression darkened. "Being a paraplegic...well, I like to dream of visiting places I know I can never go to. So, I created my own virtual reality travel agency, complete with visuals I would see if I could actually go there. Kinda stupid, isn't it?"

Hondo walked around the room and gawked at the computer consoles and workbench littered with circuit boards in various stages of completion. He turned back to Edison. "Nah," he answered. "What *is* stupid is why anyone who can build a hovering wheelchair and create high definition, 3-D images—so clear it looks like you're actually there—would think they'd be unable to visit any place on the planet."

A moment or two of silence followed. Put that way, Edison felt a glimmer of hope rise in him. *Maybe Hondo is right. Maybe the problem all along isn't my handicap, but me! Maybe the only limits are what I set on myself.* A smile slowly grew on his face.

Hondo grinned. "Who would've thought any words of wisdom would come from me, huh? Maybe I should do the tutoring!"

Edison laughed and high-fived Hondo. "Follow me," he said pointing to a work console. He swept off electrical leads, a soldering iron, and other various computer parts to clear a space. The two boys sat side by side, Hondo's math textbook and assignment in front of them.

Edison hesitated, then glanced at Hondo. "Thanks."

Puzzled, Hondo asked, "For what?"

"For being my friend."

Hondo clapped him on the back. "Okay, friend. Now help me pass math so I can play football!"

Friends.

A warm glow blossomed inside Edison. The concept less than two months ago was completely alien to him. His analytical instincts briefly kicked in and he considered the odds of how two kids so different could ever have forged a friendship. Then just as quickly, decided it really didn't matter. Some things must happen for a reason…a concept divorced from logic, and one Edison couldn't conceive of or understand just a few short weeks ago.

As he turned his attention to the first math problem on the worksheet, he decided Hondo was wrong. He wasn't rich. Not really.

Not until today.

CHAPTER 7

Edison chuckled as Hondo, wide-eyed, walked around the Olympic-sized pool.

"You've got to be kidding me! It's the size of a lake!" Hondo blurted.

The pool—located partially inside a huge solarium constructed entirely of glass—came complete with palm trees, plumeria, and other tropical floras. A flagstone path meandered through the exotic vegetation. Water cascaded from a sluice gate inside the sunroom to fall in a foaming rush to the outside-half of the pool. A concrete apron girdled the water with lounge chairs and tables grouped in strategic locations.

While Hondo continued his inspection, Edison reflected on the events of the past week. Every day after practice, Carney drove them back to the Jones Mansion where Edison continued to tutor his friend. At first, the sessions went well, but the past couple of days, Hondo seemed distracted and withdrawn, and they accomplished very little. Edison wondered if his big friend had problems with his mother's boyfriend again, but Hondo never volunteered any information and Edison was afraid to ask.

They were running out of time with the first football scrimmage against the eighth grade team set for next week. Coach Macklin reminded Hondo again if his grades didn't improve, he would be benched. To emphasize the point, the second string quarterback took half the snaps in practice. Rather than motivate Hondo, it left him angry and frustrated. The drive from practice now occurred in stony silence with none of the friendly banter that usually happened between Carney and Hondo.

Today, upon arriving, Hondo stormed straight to Edison's room without so much as a backward glance. At Carney's questioning look, Edison explained, "Coach benched him for half the practice...because of his grades."

The ex-SEAL tapped his lips. "*Hmm.* Tell you what. You boys have been going at it hard all week. Why don't you take a break from studying and do something fun for a change?"

Studying isn't fun? The thought never occurred to Edison learning might be considered work. When he suggested to Hondo they go swimming, his friend's look confirmed the burly bodyguard was right.

Wearing one of Carney's swimming trunks, Hondo ran up to the pool and shouted, "Cannonball!" He launched himself into the air. Tucking his legs beneath him, Hondo landed in the water with a mighty splash.

Edison levered himself easily into the pool. Once in the water, he swam with fluid motion toward Hondo and stopped beside him treading water. Hondo stared in amazement.

Edison grinned. "What's the matter? You never see anyone swim before?"

"But, your legs. How—?" Hondo bit his lip. "Hey, I'm sorry," he quickly added. "I didn't mean to—"

"It's okay," Edison cut in. "Swimming is one of the first things Carney taught me to do. I feel more at home in the water. The buoyancy helps to support my body, so it's easy. I bet I've gone a million laps in this pool."

"Well, in that case..." with a loud *whoop*, Hondo splashed

water in Edison's face. Legs and arms churning, Hondo swam away as fast as he could. Spluttering, Edison turned and with quick, efficient strokes, took off after him.

An hour later, the boys were back in Edison's room. An invigorated Hondo showed more interest in the study session than he had in days. Thirty minutes later, Hondo groaned and slammed his math textbook shut.

"Can't you just give me the answers?" he asked for what seemed to Edison like the hundredth time.

"Look, I've explained this to you over and over. Even *if* I gave you all the answers, how will you know how to work these problems on the test? What's more, I've looked at your average. If you don't pass your next math test, you fail for the term and will be ineligible to play football."

A few tense moments passed between the two boys before Hondo suddenly snapped his fingers.

"Hey, I know! You can fix me up with one of your high tech devices." He leaped up. "How about a pair of glasses like spies wear or like in superhero movies? You can send me the answers and they'll scroll across the lens so I can read 'em!"

Edison groaned. "In the first place, that's cheating. In the second place, even if I helped you cheat, we don't have the same math class, so how would I know which problems would be on the test? And finally, how will you learn anything about math if you don't study and do it yourself?"

"You sound like Bree!" Hondo retorted. "And lots of kids cheat and get away with it all the time."

"So what?" Edison answered, his voice rising. "It doesn't

make it right, and besides, the result is the same. You don't learn *anything!*"

Hondo glared at Edison. "You think I care whether or not I learn how to reduce a fraction? Look, the only reason I'm here is so I can play football. So yeah, if cheating helps me do that, then count me in!"

Edison picked up the closed math textbook, then flipped it back onto the desk. He backed his anti-grav chair away from Hondo. Frustrated and angry with his friend's attitude, he took several deep breaths to settle himself.

"I'll help you anyway I can," he managed to say. "You're my friend and…and while I know I have a lot to learn about what friendship is all about, it seems to me a real friend wouldn't do anything to hurt their friend. If I help you cheat, it might benefit you a little now, but in the long run, you'll have to take more tests…lots of them! You can't cheat on all of them, so what will you do then?"

Hondo didn't answer and stalked about the room, fists clenched. Abruptly, he sat down on the edge of Edison's bed, eyes rimmed with tears.

"You know what it's like to come home and find your mother passed out drunk or stoned on the floor?" he whispered. "Or to get beat up by some son of a bitch boyfriend because I moved his can of beer? When I get home, I don't think of homework, or whether or not I get a passing grade. I just think of surviving. You get that, Edison? *Surviving!*"

Hondo roughly swiped his eyes with the back of his hand. "You have all of this. You don't know what it is like to have no one, no one at all to look out for you."

Agitated, Hondo got up and stalked about the room again. "Football is my ticket outta here. It's the one thing—the *only* thing—I'm good at. If I can't play, then I've got nothing. *Nothing!*"

A weight settled on Edison's shoulders. Seeing his friend like this saddened him in ways he could hardly have imagined. With a sigh, he rotated the hoverchair to face Hondo. "You're wrong, Hondo. Remember, you were the one who told me how stupid it was to limit myself. You can do whatever you put your mind to, just like you told me."

A sudden thought struck him. "And I know what it's like to be alone. The funny thing is, I didn't realize how alone until I started going to school and met you, Bree, and Carly. For the first time, I had friends, real people, kids my age, not servants or a Siri voice from a data device. Oh, and one more thing."

"What?" Hondo snapped.

"I know what it's like not to have a mother or a father."

CHAPTER 8

Seconds ticked by. Edison sat quietly while his friend stared at him.

Hondo's anger melted away. "I'm sorry. I-I didn't know," he finally said.

Edison sighed. "It's okay. Don't worry about it." Until today, he never gave his isolation much thought, but it dawned on him his seclusion was so complete, even his friends at school knew little of his background and family.

It's time to change that.

Edison motioned to Hondo. "C'mon. I've got something to show you." He put his palm flat against an opaque screen inset within the wall. A thin line of red light scrolled back and forth and scanned his handprint. With a whisper of sound, a section of the wall parted to reveal a brightly lit, oval interior.

Hondo whistled and moved in for a closer inspection. He looked back and asked, "What's this?"

"A pneumatic elevator car. Follow me." Edison moved his anti-grav chair into the elevator. He pulled down a padded bench recessed in the interior wall and motioned for Hondo to sit in it. Edison then positioned his hoverchair beside a side panel of the car. A pair of clamps extended from the wall and fastened to the chair with a metallic *snap*. Both boys fastened their seatbelts.

"Level 20," Edison commanded.

The doors shut, and the elevator moved sideways, then dropped with stomach-clenching speed. A soft hiss whispered in the air, and the car picked up speed.

"Wh-what's happening? What is this?" Hondo babbled.

"The elevator car moves by differences in air pressure," Edison explained. "The track or shaft is hermetically sealed. By pumping air in or out of the shaft, the elevator is *pushed* or *pulled* depending on direction. The ascent or descent is smoother and uses less energy than a traditional elevator."

"You know a lot about how this elevator works, huh?" Hondo quipped while he maintained an iron grip on his seat.

Edison grinned. "I ought to. I designed it."

The car *chimed*, slowed to a complete stop, and the doors slid open. Edison released the clamps on his hoverchair, then slipped into the seat and moved out of the elevator. He motioned for Hondo, who unfastened his seatbelt and exited the car. Edison grinned at Hondo's reaction. His friend looked around, wide-eyed.

They stood in a large open room with concrete walls, ceiling, and floor. Roughly half the size of a football field, the cavernous area was brightly lit with powerful LED lights fixed to the ceiling forty feet above their heads. A number of work stations lined one wall. Each contained an assembly area with machinery and automated robotic arms. These cubicle-assembly areas were crammed with electronic components in various stages of completion.

They moved deeper into the huge workroom which included only one other door, an EXIT sign mounted above it. Not far away was an oblong object the size of a dumpster.

Hondo pointed. "What's that?" A ghostly echo of his question bounced off the walls of the enormous facility.

Edison grinned. "A robotic forklift I designed. It's made of titanium steel and can lift and move objects up to a metric ton in mass, although I generally use it for smaller objects. The manipulative arms have multiple functions and can do everything from gripping a pallet to welding steel. It runs off of a hydrogen fuel cell. Here, I'll show you."

He enabled the controls on his tablet, and with a mechanical *clank*, the forklift came to life.

Lights blazed from the cab, a low *hum* filled the air, and the forklift rose into the air. Panels on either side of the mechanism slid open, and a pair of metal appendages appeared. Extending upward into the air like lobster claws, they rotated and snapped. A recessed Duroplast shell glided up to form a clear bubble over an operator's station at the top of the forklift. Silently, it turned and traveled across the floor to stop beside the two boys.

"The forklift travels by floating on a cushion of air, or if it's carrying a heavy object, it moves like this." Edison brushed the touchscreen, and a *whirr* emanated from the base of the mechanism. Treads emerged to lift the forklift several feet off the floor. Moving the machine back and forth, Edison abruptly turned to Hondo. "Here, you take over." He handed the tablet to his friend.

Hesitant, Hondo took the controller. With Edison's coaching, he cautiously moved the machine around the huge workroom. Picking up empty crates with the robotic arms, he stacked them on top of each other.

Hondo laughed. "Hey, this ain't so hard! Playing all those video games finally came in handy!" After a few more minutes, Edison took the controls back and powered down the forklift.

Edison followed after Hondo, content to let his friend wander about his underground lab. They came to a section of the workroom where he kept a wooden desk, and an old-fashioned swivel chair. Plain and without adornment, only a single framed picture rested on the desk's worn wooden surface.

"What's this beat up desk and old chair doing here?" Hondo asked. "Everything else in here is high tech." He picked up the frame and studied the family picture—a mother, father, and a small boy. His eyes widened at the sight. "Is that you and your parents?" he asked.

Edison nodded. "They were killed in a car accident, murdered actually, and the same accident left me like this."

Hondo's mouth fell open. "What? Murdered?"

Edison opened one of the desk's drawers and pulled out a thick notebook. He flipped it open and showed it to his friend. He turned the laminated pages one after another, each containing newspaper articles and a variety of pictures taken from different angles of a crumpled SUV. In one gruesome scene, the entire front of the vehicle was folded together in an accordion-like mass of metal, the passenger-side partially sheared off as if pared by a giant knife. The next laminated sheet revealed a pair of zipped body bags being loaded into a coroner's van.

The look of shock on Hondo's face brought a lump to Edison's throat. The same images always left his emotions raw and unsettled. "There's other pages with accident and coroner reports if you want to see them too."

Hondo shook his head and closed the folder. "Ah, that's okay. I've seen enough." He asked, "What happened? Why did you say your parents were murdered?"

Edison shoved the notebook back in the drawer. His hands clutched the hoverchair's arms, and his nostrils flared. "My father and grandpa were perfecting a cold fusion process, one which they said could produce unlimited amounts of energy with virtually no carbon imprint or other contaminants to harm the environment. Our company, LogicTech, didn't intend to patent the discovery. Rather, they both agreed the impact of such a discovery would so revolutionize life on our planet, that it had to be shared freely. Somehow, word leaked out about what LogicTech intended to do, and someone decided they had to be stopped."

Hondo blurted, "What? Why would anyone do that?"

With a bitter shake of his head, Edison said, "Money and lots of it, not to mention the influence a company, an individual, or even a country could wield if they controlled the fusion process. So, there were lots of people who wanted the secret of cold fusion. And if they couldn't have it, they were just as determined to keep it out of the hands of everyone else."

"So, you mean the car accident...wasn't an accident?"

"Yes. My grandpa was supposed to be in the car with us, but a last minute emergency came up. I don't remember much about what happened other than the car suddenly sped up, left the highway, and plowed into a roadside embankment. The next thing I remember was waking up in a hospital bed and my legs wouldn't move."

"Well, what happened to this, er, 'cold fusion' stuff you said your dad worked on?"

Edison snorted. "My grandpa shut the project down at once. He mothballed the research facility and had the data encrypted."

Hondo blinked. "Huh? Why? Didn't he want to finish what your father started?"

The question hung in the air.

Edison jaw clenched, finally answered. "Because I lived."

Hondo stared. "Huh? Because you lived?"

Arms crossed, Edison shook his head. "I could never get Grandpa to tell me why he closed the project. One day, I cornered Carney and threatened to hack into the company's mainframe and find out myself if he didn't tell me. Basically, he said Grandpa did it to protect me. He believed if the cold fusion project continued, the people who murdered my parents would try to get at him through me. He wasn't willing to take the risk, so he shut the whole thing down—permanently."

"Wow! That's some really bad stuff," Hondo breathed. "I'm sorry, dude."

Edison stared, a distant look on his face. When he turned back to Hondo, his expression hardened. "One day I'm going to finish what my father started—and no one will stop me!"

Hondo fiddled with the old leather seat, pushing it back and forth.

"The chair, the desk, it all belonged to my father," Edison explained. "Grandpa told me my dad, even though he was the chief software designer for LogicTech, loved old-fashioned things like antique furniture. He said my father told him it helped keep him 'rooted' to what really mattered in life."

Hondo pointed at the framed photo on the desk. "Is that why you keep your family's picture here? So you'll stay 'rooted' too?"

Edison didn't answer. Finally, in a quiet voice, he said, "I'm starting to forget what my parents looked like. Even the time we had together before the crash is fading. I thought if I put the desk, chair, and picture here, it would help me to focus, to remember."

Hondo plopped into the ancient chair, its wheels squealing from the sudden weight. "Be glad you have things worth remembering. Me, I don't think about the past at all. Just what's gonna happen in the future."

He rapped the top of the desk with his knuckles. "You know, you still haven't told me."

Edison quirked an eyebrow. "Told you what?"

"Where we are, and what this place is."

CHAPTER 9

EDISON LAUGHED, AND THE SOMBER MOOD DISSIPATED.

"Well, to begin with, we are twenty stories underground, and this is my lab or workshop. This is where I work on my projects, everything from micro-circuit boards to trial models like the robotic forklift. I usually spend most of my time here…at least I did until I started junior high school."

"Twenty stories underground?" Hondo blurted.

The look on Hondo's face caused another chuckle from Edison. He manipulated tabs on the touchscreen of his tablet, and a 3-D holograph projected in mid-air between the two boys.

"Forty years ago, this place, including the Jones Mansion and the surrounding area, used to be strip-mined for lignite coal." The holographic image showed an aerial view of mountains of earth piled high by a gargantuan crane exposing coal seams. Massive trenches scarred the landscape, bucket after bucket of earth being removed from above the veins of coal. Smaller cranes, dwarfed by their much larger cousin, worked tirelessly to load the coal into the beds of hauler dump trucks.

"By federal law, this land must be reclaimed once the mining operations cease. Then, the land has to be held and maintained for at least twenty years by the mining company before it can be released for public sale."

The holograph showed a vista of pastures, trees, and ponds which dotted the landscape in pastels of green and blue.

"You mean all this was strip-mined land?"

Edison nodded. "That's when Grandpa stepped in. LogicTech does a lot of work for the Department of Defense, much of it top secret. He brokered an agreement with the federal government which allowed LogicTech to purchase ten square miles of strip-mined land before reclamation and the public auction."

Hondo frowned. "Why?"

"So he could do *this*."

A tap on the tablet caused the 3-D image to change to another view. In this one, the giant crane, rather than moving earth to expose a coal seam, worked to make the excavation wider and deeper! The scene then altered again to display a massive excavation pit filled with an army of construction workers and cement trucks. Smaller trenches, arrayed like spokes on a wheel, emanated from the central excavation site and ended in smaller quarry pits complete with individual construction crews.

The images jumped ahead in time, and instead of ragged earth at the bottom of a deep pit, a row of squat buildings laid out in geometric fashion appeared. Composed of thick walls of smooth, gray concrete, the entire structure resembled a child's building blocks—only these "blocks" were gigantic in size and connected with a maze of hardened tunnels.

A final scene appeared. The massive crane now moved the raw earth taken from the mine, and refilled the excavation covering up the buildings and construction site.

"Whoa!" Hondo cried. "All those buildings are being buried under dirt!"

Edison grinned. "Correct. Now it looks like this." The holograph displayed a landscape of rolling pastures, groves of pine trees, and scattered ponds.

Hondo scratched his head. "You mean this is where that gigantic hole used to be?"

"Yep. You saw the construction of LogicTech's main research facility. It opened ten years ago."

"But why bury it?"

Edison shrugged. "Simple really. As I said, LogicTech does a lot of top secret work for the government. Strip-mined land is cheap, and a buried research annex twenty stories deep makes industrial espionage almost impossible. With fixed entry and exit locations, this insures the entire complex remains isolated and secure. Even microwaves would have difficulty penetrating this far. It's also economical. The layers of soil insulate the facility and lower the cost of heating and cooling."

Edison tapped the touchscreen and the visual images disappeared. "LogicTech has been rated one of the top environmentally friendly companies in the world," he said proudly. "The company has continued the land reclamation and maintenance over and above what is required by law. Grandpa believes this is one of the major missions and purposes of the corporation...to leave the world a better place."

Edison rotated the anti-grav chair. "So, what do you think? Now you know all about me and my family."

Eyes twinkling, Hondo said, "I think you're the only kid I know with his own underground lab...and I *still* need to pass math to play football."

Edison cast a shrewd glance at his friend. "Does this mean you are ready to study?"

Hondo picked up the Jones family picture and studied it again. He placed it back on the desk.

"Yeah...I think I am."

CHAPTER 10

"So, do you think Hondo passed his test?" Bree asked as she and Edison exited the cafeteria. They headed toward a tree-lined plaza where many other students were already congregated.

Before Edison could answer, Carly shot out of a cluster of brightly-clad cheerleaders and caught up with them.

"I mean, Hondo's got to pass!" she gushed. "Our first pep rally is last period, and the cheer outfits this year are *so* cute!" She spun in a pirouette to show off her red, black, and white cheer ensemble.

"Hondo has to be able to play so he can see me cheer for him!" Carly continued. She pulled Bree by the arm and giggled into her ear. "Isn't he so cute? He's such a hunk."

Bree rolled her eyes. "Carly, you're supposed to support the entire football team, not just Hondo."

Carly flipped her hand. "Oh, everyone knows if Hondo is ineligible, the team won't win a game." As if that settled the matter, she tugged Bree close again. "I can't wait for the game!" Her enthusiasm was infectious, and soon, both girls were giggling.

Edison, a forgotten spectator, was grateful Carly became distracted by her focus on Hondo. For some reason, he always got tongue-tied around Carly, a frustrating puzzle he couldn't unravel. With other friends like Bree and Hondo, he never had that problem.

Why did Carly pose such a challenge for him?

Deep in thought, he didn't pay close attention to where he was going, and his hoverchair collided with a thick pair of legs.

"Watch where you're going!" a voice snarled.

Before Edison could move, his hoverchair was savagely shoved backward. Edison's head snapped forward, and only a quick adjustment of the controls prevented the anti-grav chair from ramming into Bree and Carly.

Edison shook his head to clear it, and got his first look at the source of the voice's face. His heart sank.

Markie Franks.

Even though new to the school, Edison was well aware of the bully's reputation. In the entire seventh grade, only Hondo was bigger than Franks. Bree informed him that Markie was older than everyone because he failed the fifth grade.

Franks' wide body came with large meaty hands and stocky arms and legs. A block of a head with a pit-bull face, rested on broad, square shoulders. The bully's disposition, much like a pit-bull's, had been witnessed by Edison on several occasions.

Franks and his posse of friends liked to stalk the hallways and the school grounds, the students parting fearfully to let them pass. Those too timid or slow found themselves shoved into a wall or locker, often with an added bonus of a kick or punch.

Markie Franks was the last person Edison wanted to run into.

Cruel eyes squinted at Edison from below a pair of thick, ridged brows. "Hey, crip, are you blind too?" Franks jeered. Snorts of derision echoed from his friends who surrounded Edison. Like pilot fish, they attached themselves to Markie, following him wherever he went.

"I-I'm so-sorry," Edison stammered. "I didn't mean to run into you."

A spark of recognition appeared in the bully's eyes. "Hey, I know you! You're the rich kid with the fancy wheelchair! The one who lives in the big mansion north of town."

With a harsh laugh, Franks pointed at Edison. "Don't look like all your money could buy you a new set of legs though, does it?" Howls of laughter erupted from his gang, and the hoverchair was roughly jostled as they closed into an even tighter circle.

Edison's face flushed, his heart beating a tattoo in his chest. Suddenly, Carly and Bree pushed their way through the human cordon around him.

Carly shook her finger at Markie. "You leave him alone!" she cried. Her face reflected cold rage in sharp contrast to the giggling girl from only moments earlier.

"You bully! You better back off!" Bree hurled at Franks. She joined Carly and they stood, arms crossed, beside Edison.

Edison stared in amazement at the transformation of both girls. He had never seen Carly mad, and soft-spoken Bree looked like she could rip Markie's face off with her bare hands!

Undaunted, Franks snorted and looked the girls up and down. His eyes lingered insolently on Carly.

"Tell you what," he said with a leer, "if you want to be a nursemaid for this gimp, that's fine with me. I'll meet you someplace after school and we can have a nice, long talk about it…along with more interesting things." He jerked his thumb at Bree. "As for this bag of bones, you'll have to leave her behind."

More raucous laughter rang out into the air. Abruptly, a large hand reached out and grabbed one of Markie's gang by the collar, hurling him backwards. Moments later, Hondo shoved through the space and stepped past Edison. He shouldered Carly and Bree behind him, and came to a stop with his nose inches from Markie, a dangerous smile on his face.

"You know, you're an even uglier bastard up close, Franks," Hondo snorted. "And I didn't think that was possible." An instant silence fell, the crowd of students watching the two boys eye each other malevolently.

"This is none of your business, Edwards." Markie sneered. "I suggest you move your ass somewhere else before I move it for you."

"Can't do that, Franks. See, Edison is my friend, and I can't let a pussy like you go around picking on help—I mean, disadvantaged friends."

Although Hondo caught himself, Edison knew he almost said "helpless". The realization made the confrontation with Markie pale in comparison.

His humiliation had now come full circle.

A loud voice interrupted his dark thoughts. "What's going on here? Break it up!" Coach Watson, the boys' basketball coach, and the assistant principal, Wallace Dirks, pushed their way through the knot of students. At the sight of both men, students melted away, mumbling at being denied the live entertainment.

"Markie! Can't you stay out of trouble? Who are you picking on now?" Although phrased as a question, Wallace Dirks mouthed it as a statement of fact. Beefy and wide, the former football player and coach had bright, red hair clipped close to his scalp, a match for a face flushed with anger.

"That you, Hondo?" Coach Watson asked. Tall and slender, his chiseled, angular face peered at Hondo in disapproval. "Don't you have a scrimmage today? How are you going to play if you are in detention?"

Hondo wore an innocent expression. "We were just talking about the scrimmage, Coach." He clapped Franks so hard on the shoulder it brought a grimace to the bully's face. "Right, Markie?"

"Yeah, sure. We were talking about the game."

He shrugged off Hondo's hand. A cunning glint appeared in his eyes. "You know, I really like football. I might come to *all* the games this year!" Markie glanced at Hondo, and for a moment, their eyes locked.

Franks finally broke eye contact. He turned to Wallace Dirks. "Can, I go now?"

Dirks pointed at Edison, then Carly and Bree. "What about it? Anything happen?"

Hondo shot them a look, followed by a faint shake of his head.

Carly looped her arm through Bree's. "I don't think so, Mr. Dirks. Hondo and Markie were just talking." Bree looked like she swallowed a lemon, but managed to nod. When Dirks looked over at Edison, he smiled weakly and nodded also.

The assistant principal released a frustrated sigh and turned to Markie. "I've had enough of your bullying, Franks. If I get another report on you, and you'll be spending *lots* of time in detention!"

Dirks rounded on Hondo. "I'll make very sure Coach Macklin knows who you keep company with. Maybe fifty bear crawls *on* the football field will help you make better decisions *off* the field!" With that, he dismissed them with an angry wave of his hand.

Franks grunted and sauntered away. He stopped and spun to cast an insolent glance back at the group of friends. "I'll see you later, especially you two!" he added with a hard look at Edison and Hondo.

Dirks and Coach Watson missed this last exchange, and Edison grabbed Hondo's arm to stop him from going after Markie. Snickering, Franks ambled off.

Tension thrummed through Hondo's body, and Edison struggled to keep a grip on him. "Don't! It's not worth it.

Remember, you have a football game today." Carly and Bree both chimed their agreement. Edison kept a grasp on his friend until Hondo's muscles relaxed.

"Well, how did you do on your test?" he asked in an attempt to diffuse the tense atmosphere.

Hondo's face brightened. He dug into his back pocket and handed Edison a folded paper. Edison spread it out on his lap and studied it.

His eyes widened. "You made a 'B' on your six-week test. Congratulations, you passed!" Carly and Bree jumped up and down, the incident with Franks momentarily forgotten.

Edison studied the test further and frowned. "You might have made an 'A' if you answered the extra-credit questions." He handed the test back to Hondo.

"Nah. What does it matter as long as I pass? Besides, if I got an 'A', then the teacher might expect more out of me." He folded the test and put it back in his pocket. He walked off with Carly chattering in his ear.

Left alone, an awkward silence settled around Edison and Bree.

"Are you okay?" Bree asked.

"Yeah. I'm good," he lied. In truth, he'd never felt worse.

Since the accident, he struggled to overcome his disability. Although at times this proved to be difficult, he thought he had more or less succeeded. He never considered himself helpless despite the loss of the use of his legs.

Not until today.

Not only did Hondo have to intercede for him, but so did Bree and Carly. The worst part—the absolute *worst* part—was the realization that were the tables turned, he could have done nothing for them! This feeling of powerlessness left him numb.

Sensing his frustration, Bree placed her hand on his shoulder.

"You know, friends look out for each other. That's what friends do."

Edison gazed at Bree, struck by her perception. So far, most of the seventh-graders he met couldn't think one minute past the end of their nose. Many of the boys felt there could be no higher art form than cutting a fart in the middle of class.

Bree was different.

She actually thought about things. Although she occupied the body of a twelve-year old girl, she possessed the maturity of someone at least ten tears older. He blinked in sudden realization.

She's a lot like me.

Edison patted her hand. "We better start back. The bell is going to ring, and we don't want to be late for class." They made the trek in silence, yet inside, Edison's mind churned.

He didn't know how or when, but he made a vow to himself.

I will never be helpless again.

CHAPTER 11

A PALPABLE ENERGY CRACKLED IN THE AIR.

Although only a scrimmage with just the seventh and eighth-grade teams playing each other, even Edison was excited about his first live football game. Parents and siblings jammed the bleachers, and loud cheers rose to a crescendo when both teams trotted out onto the field to begin warm-up drills. Hondo's team wore the red practice jerseys, while the eighth graders wore the home team whites.

On the sidelines, Edison prepared to videotape the scrimmage. He recognized Hondo immediately, even with his football helmet on. The largest player on the field, including the eighth grade team, he grinned and waved at Edison as he jogged to his place on the warm-up line. Edison waved in return, then glanced at the parents in the stands. *Was Hondo's mother among them?* Saddened that she probably wasn't, he returned his attention to a pocket-sized device in his hand.

Manipulating the controls, Edison caused a silver, spherical object to rise from where it rested in his lap. The size of a softball, the airborne camera hovered at eye level before he sent it zooming skyward. It stopped one hundred feet above the football field. He squinted at the monitor on the controls, then tested the resolution on the airborne video camera. Minutes later, satisfied the hovering camera functioned properly, he set the controls aside.

Edison grinned at the reaction of the fans who noticed his device. They pointed at his floating camera. Even some of the football players stopped their warm-ups and craned their necks to get a better view. Edison's grin grew wider when some of the coaches who barked at the players to resume stretching, snuck a look skyward.

When he volunteered to video all of Hondo's football games, Edison didn't realize what a maze the bleachers would be. Although there were wheelchair ramps, getting to the press-box to video the game would be impossible, even for Edison's hover-chair. It forced him to improvise from the sidelines, and provided a perfect opportunity to test an adaptation he'd been itching to try—use his anti-gravity magnet on something other than his wheelchair, and to also increase the altitude of the object!

Formatting the video camera had been easy. He simply took existing digital video technology and embedded it within the device he constructed the Anti-Gravity Magnet in. Then he synced the resolution controls to his handheld tablet. This left him with the problem of miniaturizing the AGMAG components to fit into the much smaller containment shell holding the camera. In the end, Edison built three concentric electromagnetic rings that were stacked one on top of the other. Each ring produced a cone-shaped anti-gravity field that in concert with the other electromagnets, could raise or lower the camera, or change its direction.

The two biggest problems to overcome were an energy source to power the electromagnets, and how to prevent the field they generated from wiping the data chip controller. Edison decided to use an experimental hydrogen fuel cell he developed to provide power. He wasn't sure if the miniaturized battery would last the entire football game and brought an extra one just in case. Although he developed the prototype—the fuel cell was a LogicTech product—his grandpa would not be pleased if he learned Edison used experimental technology to film a football game.

Since the placement of the electromagnets directed their energy down and away from the video camera, it created a null field in the area above. Nevertheless, Edison sandwiched a thick layer of plastic in this space to prevent any conduction which might wipe the data chip.

The game started on time, with Edison having a front row seat on the sidelines. The eighth grade won the flip, and ran the kick-off back to the forty-yard line. On the first play, Hondo—who also played linebacker—broke through the offensive line. He shrugged off one last desperate blocker and leveled the quarterback. The football squirted high in the air, and Hondo, like a cat pursuing a mouse, pounced on it.

Wild cheers shook the bleachers on the seventh grade side, while a collective groan sounded from the eighth grade fans. Hondo, the football held aloft triumphantly in one hand, spiked it into the turf before turning to trot toward his offense already huddled on the field.

The coaches signaled the play to Hondo from the sideline. He relayed the information to the offense, and the huddle broke. Settled under the center, Hondo barked the count. Receiving the snap, he kept the football on a sweep left. Racing down the sideline, he broke tackle after tackle to burst into the end zone and score the game's first touchdown. Hondo curled his right arm, pointed at his bicep, and struck a pose. He pumped his fist and hooted, his teammates mobbing him.

The roar that filled the stadium rattled the bleachers. The spectacle amazed Edison. Even the eighth-grade team's parents cheered wildly for his large friend! Basking in the adulation,

Hondo wore a wide smile, and in that moment, Edison finally realized what football meant to his friend. It filled the gaping hole formed by his dysfunctional mother and her abusive boyfriends... just like his inventions filled the void left when his parents were killed.

Happy for Hondo, Edison's gaze fell upon Carly, the head cheerleader. She led an enthusiastic routine of backflips and shaking pom-poms. At the end of the cheer, she turned to look down the sideline at Hondo. A sharp pang of jealousy coursed through Edison, and he silently raged against the unfairness of his condition.

He took several deep breaths to calm himself. A conversation he had with his grandpa years earlier came back to him—as it always did when he felt sorry for himself. "Life isn't about being fair," Stanton Jones told him. "Bad things happen to good people all the time. Life is about *how* you take those circumstances and *what* you do with them."

Edison recalled with crystal clarity what happened next. His grandpa gripped him firmly by both shoulders and looked him straight in the eye. "The accident took your legs, Edison, but it didn't take your mind, and it didn't take your spirit. God has given you extraordinary gifts, so use them, and don't ever look back."

They were hard words for Stanton Jones to say, and Edison could still see the glint of tears in his eyes while he spoke. But, they were also necessary words, and Edison, even at his tender age, understood what his grandpa meant.

Since then, he tried very hard to never feel sorry for himself again.

Sometimes, he couldn't help his feelings. When he gazed at Carly, he felt an emotional tug he was completely unprepared for.

Why are my thoughts so jumbled around Carly but not with Bree and other girls? It's hard for me to even complete a sentence around her.

He swallowed. *Best get back to the game.* Fortuitously, a roar came from the crowd as the seventh-grade team kicked off. Gratified to have something to occupy his mind, Edison returned his attention to the camera's controls.

The final score, 38-7, completed a blowout by the younger seventh-grade team. Hondo rushed for three touchdowns, passed for one more, and had been a terror from his linebacker position. He sacked the quarterback six times, and also made numerous tackles of the running backs. Pulled for the second string quarterback in the fourth quarter, he watched the rest of the game from the sidelines. Edison overheard numerous parents and fans comment on how Hondo was the best young football player they had ever seen.

After the game, Carney congratulated Hondo as the last of the fans and parents streamed by. A huge grin on his face, Hondo paused before leaving to shower and get dressed. He pointed at Edison.

"The first touchdown was because of you."

"Huh? What do you mean?"

"The first play we did a sweep left. Don't you remember your 'analysis' of our practices? That we averaged more yards per carry on the left side? Thanks, buddy!" Hondo saluted and trotted off.

Mouth open, Edison turned to Carney. "You mean they actually used it in their plays?"

Carney laughed. "I think you've given the term 'scouting report' a whole new meaning. Congratulations!" Edison couldn't keep the broad grin off his face.

He helped the team score a touchdown!

Edison followed his bodyguard to the parking lot. He slid onto the front seat of the Mercedes, but before he could shut the door, a burst of raucous laughter came from nearby. He turned his head in the direction of the commotion. Markie Franks stood by one of the bleacher exits, a number of his followers scattered beside him. He pointed at Edison. With a fresh round of laughter, he turned and sauntered by the front of the sedan, his posse close behind.

Carney frowned at the stricken look on Edison's face. "What's wrong?" He gestured at the cluster of boys walking by. "Those guys bothering you?"

The question hung in the air as Edison struggled to control his fear. The vow he made to himself rang out in his mind. *I'll never be helpless again!*

He turned back toward Carney, his chin set with steely determination. "No, but thanks for asking." Edison felt the ex-SEAL's eyes study him before he put the car in gear and pulled out of the parking lot.

Edison was grateful they were finally headed home.

CHAPTER 12

Edison stopped his hoverchair and gestured to Hondo. "This is the place."

They stood in a large clearing a couple of hundred yards from the Jones Mansion. Groves of pine trees surrounded the grassy meadow and the sharp smell of sap floated in the air. Hondo picked up a pine cone and hurled it into the trees. "This is what you wanted to show me?"

The seventh-grade football team won their first district game the night before in resounding fashion, 40-6. Hondo had been magnificent, passing for two touchdowns and rushing for two more. Because they played so well, Coach Macklin gave the team the Friday practice off.

Hondo came home with Edison and later abruptly asked to spend the night. When Carney asked if it was okay with his mother, Hondo shrugged and said he would call her. He used Edison's cell phone and left a curt voice mail, *"I'm at Edison's."*

Edison grinned and pointed. "No. *That* is." Although late in the evening with the autumn sun low in the horizon, the dwindling light clearly revealed a tall object covered with a tarp.

Hondo's face brightened. "Hey! What's that?"

Edison chuckled and pulled the tarp off to reveal a male mannequin dressed in camouflaged fatigues.

"Hondo, meet Bob the Mannequin. Bob, meet Hondo!"

Walking up to the mannequin, Hondo grabbed a molded plastic hand and pumped it vigorously. "Pleased to meet you!"

Hondo glanced at Edison. "I don't guess Bob is going to tell us why he's out here in the middle of a field, is he?"

"Well, if he could talk, Bob would tell us he's going to be part of a test," Edison quipped.

Edison moved his hoverchair back fifty feet. "This ought to be far enough."

A latched case, the size of a small suitcase, rested in his lap. He opened it, and inside sat a heavy, metallic-grey object. It glinted in the weak light as Edison pulled it out and examined it. Constructed of a bulbous barrel which tapered into a small cylindrical opening, the barrel was attached to a thick grip with a trigger. Mounted below the barrel was a smaller cylinder covered in a thick layer of insulating rubber. A scope rested on top of the larger barrel, and a stock, made of metal and plastic with a thick foam rubber pad, extended from the back of the object. Spring-loaded to absorb shock, the stock fit snugly against Edison's shoulder.

Hondo leaned over and squinted at the mysterious object. "What's that?" he blurted. "It looks like a cross between a power drill and a gun."

"You're not too far off the mark," Edison replied. "It's actually called a vortex cannon."

Hondo crowded closer. "Cannon? Cool! How's it work?"

Edison pointed at the augmented barrel. "Air or gas is forced into this chamber. A piston located at the back of the cylinder forces the air out of the shaft with explosive force. This in turn creates a vortex or shock wave which travels faster than the speed of sound."

Hondo gestured at the smaller cylinder attached below the barrel. "So what's that for?"

"It contains liquid hydrogen, a *noble* gas. At room temperature, it expands rapidly from a liquid to a gas."

Edison pressed a button below a small LED screen mounted above the grip. A *hum* emanated from the vortex cannon and thumbing the button again, Edison caused the whine to increase in pitch. A digital display appeared on the screen.

"The readout on the monitor ranges from green to red," Edison explained. "Anything in the green means the vortex wave being created is within the tolerance limit of the cannon's design. Anything in the red means the wave has reached the structural limits of the cannon...basically, you don't want to go there."

"Why? What will happen?"

"It could...well, it could explode," Edison admitted.

Hondo jerked back. "What? Explode? No way!"

"I've tested it multiple times, and I have built-in redundancies to make sure it doesn't happen," Edison quickly assured him. "Besides, the stress limits are actually rated higher than they appear when in the red zone. I've exploded several—"

"Wait! You've blown up this thing? Where?" Hondo blurted.

"I built a containment chamber in my lab. It's similar to what the army uses to detonate and dispose of portable IEDs."

"Cool!" Hondo gushed. "How come you didn't invite me when you blew stuff up?"

Edison laughed. "I'm not sure Coach Macklin would approve of you becoming involved in any experiment which produces explosions."

Crestfallen, Hondo said, "I guess you're right. What does Carney and your grandfather think about your experiments?"

Edison's face flushed, and he stammered, "Uh, well...I kinda haven't told them yet. It's probably best if we keep this, you know, a secret."

Hondo grinned. "Gotcha!"

Edison rubbed his hands together. "So, are you ready to help me test the vortex cannon?"

"You kidding? Let's go!"

Holding the barrel in front of him, Edison squinted through the sight. "The scope automatically finds the range and adjusts the output of the cannon. All you do is point and pull the trigger. Unfortunately, the range is somewhat limited because of the nature of the shock wave being created. The waves disperse and spread out the farther away from the muzzle they travel. Therefore, accuracy becomes problematic after fifty feet or so."

Hondo stared at Edison. "I guess I'm going to have Alexa translate for me when we have these talks. Remember, I'm a kid! Not one of your grandfather's engineers."

Heat warmed Edison's face. "Oh. Sorry."

Hondo waved him off. "It's okay. So let me see if I got this right. Any target past fifty feet, the vortex cannon can't hit squat."

Relieved, Edison nodded. He pointed at the insulated cylinder under the barrel. "That's why I added the liquid hydrogen. A small amount is released within the chamber to give the vortex wave a little added mass, uh, I mean kick, so when the wave travels from the muzzle, it retains its integrity, or, ah, its substance or form, longer."

Hondo's eyes glowed. "What are we waiting for? Let's put Bob to the test!"

After a last minute power check, Edison set the intensity level, sighted once more through the scope, and pulled the trigger.

A loud *pop* rang out like a cork pulled from the world's largest champagne bottle. A shiver vibrated through the air, and a split-second later, Bob the Mannequin shook violently as if a strong gust of wind suddenly blew by.

"Awesome!" Hondo cried and ran to inspect the dummy. Breathless, he turned and asked, "Can I try?"

With a grin, Edison handed his friend the vortex cannon. After another demonstration on its operation, he sat back while Hondo sighted and pulled the trigger. Another tremor passed through the air, and the mannequin rocked back and forth.

"Dude, that's frickin' awesome!" Hondo howled.

After several more blasts from the cannon, some at closer and farther distances, Hondo turned to Edison with a mischievous gleam in his eye. "Let's dial it up as far as it will go and see what happens!"

Edison scratched his ear. "I don't know. We ought to be careful until I have thoroughly tested it."

"You've already tested it! Besides, you said the design limits were actually higher than the red zone readings."

Edison thought for a moment before he gave a reluctant nod. "Okay. But I'm limiting the power output to just barely in the red zone."

"Sure." Hondo tapped his foot while Edison reset the controls and then handed him the cannon. Bouncing on his toes, he pointed it at Bob and pulled the trigger.

A concussive sound, much louder and with a *crack* like thunder rather than the normal *pop*, filled the air. Hondo, the stock firmly against his shoulder, was staggered by the kick and driven back a step. Bob's clothing was blown off and sailed high into the air, some of it coming to rest in the crowns of the pine trees adjacent to the clearing. The mannequin, propelled backwards by the force of the shock wave, came to rest ten feet away with Bob's head digging a furrow into the soil.

Whooping and waving the vortex cannon over his head, Hondo ran to the dummy and pulled it back to an upright position. Edison hurried to join him.

Grinning from ear-to-ear, Hondo said, "Looks like good ol' Bob is going to need some new clothes."

The horizon, awash in brilliant hues of gold and red, signaled the last ebb of sunset. The boys reluctantly turned to leave the denuded mannequin and make their way back to the mansion.

"Why did you build this cannon?" Hondo asked as he trudged alongside Edison's anti-grav chair.

Edison remained silent then abruptly stopped and faced his friend. "I wanted something I could use to help me if I have any, you know, disagreements with other people. Something which won't hurt anybody, but would at the same time stop them from harassing me."

Hondo frowned and scratched his cheek. "Why would anybody have a problem—"

His eyes widened and he snapped his fingers. "Franks!" he spat. "You're doing this because of Markie Franks! Look, just say the word and I'll make sure—"

"No!" Edison cried cutting him off. "You don't understand. I'm doing this for *me*! The world is full of kids like Markie Franks, and I can't have you or anyone else always fighting my battles. I have to do this. I have to learn to take care of myself!"

Edison could tell his friend was taken aback by his outburst. Quietly he added, "That's why we were testing the vortex cannon. I plan to outfit my hoverchair with them. But I have to make sure of the power settings so I don't hurt anyone…and I wanted you to know why."

Hondo's mouth opened and closed several times. Finally, he threw his arms up. "Okay. Do it your way. But don't forget I've got your back, anytime and anywhere." With that, both boys resumed their trek back to the mansion.

Edison, although grateful for Hondo's offer, was relieved he agreed to let Edison handle any future incidents with Markie Franks on his own. Nevertheless, his big friend's unequivocal support caused a warm glow to grow within him. Bree's words floated through his mind.

That's what friends are for.

CHAPTER 13

Edison's mind was on cruise control as he navigated the crowded school hallway.

Both he and Hondo had been invited to a party at Carly's house after the varsity football game Friday night. At first, he had been excited until Hondo told him it was a Wii party with a Wii dance competition. Edison's heart immediately sank, and now he regretted telling Carly he would come. While everyone else danced, he would watch from his hoverchair—alone and by himself.

Preoccupied, he ran various excuses through his mind to tell Carly he couldn't go, when his anti-grav chair was slammed violently against the wall of the hallway. Dazed, he looked up, and Markie Franks' leering face swam into his vision.

"Hey, watch where you're going!"

Before Edison could reply, Franks, gave his anti-grav chair another hard push, and laughing, turned and walked away, his posse taking up position alongside him. Everything went quiet like a giant pause button had been hit, as students stopped to see what happened. As Franks walked off, the pause button released, and students continued their hurried rush to class, the normal noise and chatter resuming.

Edison, lips set in a grim line, watched Franks saunter away.

Since the incident with the bully in the commons area two weeks earlier, a string of "accidental" collisions occurred and grew more frequent. Sometimes it involved members of Franks' gang, and sometimes it involved the large bully himself. He was too cunning to have these incidents occur within sight of a teacher or administrator, and none happened when Bree, Carly, or Hondo were with Edison. He told no one, not even Carney or his grandpa about the harassment, content instead to bide his time.

He had a plan.

He checked his cell phone. *Another hour before lunch.* Barring any unforeseen circumstances, that's when he would launch his scheme. A tingle traveled up his spine.

I can't wait!

Brrring!

Edison had his anti-grav chair on the move before the last echo of the bell died. He immediately became lost amongst the sea of students as he shot out of the classroom. Turning, he made his way down the hallway to the exit.

Edison passed several of the Markie's posse on his way out. He gave each of them his best imitation of an insolent smile, even going so far as to point and laugh at them. He practiced in front of a mirror for an hour the night before until he felt he had perfected the look. His facial muscles still ached at the unusual way in which he stretched them. At any rate, Edison had no doubt they would immediately report his actions to Franks. In fact, he was counting on it.

It was all part of his plan.

Once out the main doors of the junior high building, instead of going to the cafeteria, Edison turned left and slowly made his way through the commons area. He wanted to make it easy for anyone to follow him. Convinced Markie's gang tracked his movements, he hid a smile.

Exactly what I wanted.

Edison traveled farther away from the main concourse, the number of students thinning out until he found himself alone. He turned the corner and recognized the isolated area between the main gymnasium and the smaller, auxiliary gym. As expected, it lay deserted. Tunnel-like, the narrow surface between the two buildings consisted of poured concrete with storm drains interspersed on either side. Although a favorite place for skateboarders, the scattering of cigarette butts initially drew Edison's interest. Their stubbed-out remains were the reason he had chosen this isolated place.

Markie Franks and his posse liked to hang out here.

Edison had hacked into the school's security camera system and spent the greater part of the past two weeks following the movements of Franks and his fellow goons. Harpersville's security system stored digital images for up to six months, so once in the system, it had been no problem to access the digital library. Edison soon learned why Franks picked this very spot. Like many security systems, blind spots existed. The corner between the two gyms contained such an area and did not show up on any video images. His study showed Markie took a circuitous route and arrived at this spot with no school administrator being the wiser.

Edison positioned himself carefully so he faced the corner between the two gyms. Once situated, he did a final systems check. Satisfied everything was in the green, he settled down to wait. He hadn't been there long when Franks swept into the alley, his followers spreading out beside him.

A wolfish smile appeared on Franks' face. "This *is* my lucky day. What are the odds we would both end up here during lunch at the same time?"

He looked around. "Doesn't look like you have that pussy, Edwards, or any girls to hold your hand. And here I thought you're supposed to be some kind of genius, but now you're all alone. I mean, I know you're a gimp, but are you just plain stupid too?" His gang found this hilarious, and their laughter echoed off the walls.

Although his heart raced, Edison managed to keep a calm appearance. "No coincidence, Franks. I knew you would follow me here, and I don't need any of my friends to help me. It's time we had it out."

Markie's mouth dropped, but he quickly recovered. "I'm shaking in my boots, Jones. What are you going to do, talk me to death?"

"I hoped you would leave me alone, that's all. Just leave me alone. If you don't…then I'm prepared to defend myself."

Markie's eyes narrowed in suspicion. "What is this, some kind of a joke? You think because you're in a wheelchair I won't kick your ass? Because if you do, here's a newsflash. As far as I'm concerned, you're just a rich kid who thinks because you got money, you're better than me. Better than us!" He gestured to his gang.

Franks balled his hand into a large fist. "Let's see if your money can stop this." He stalked toward Edison.

Edison barked, "Hold it, Franks!" Markie stopped and blinked at Edison's sudden outburst.

"What?" he snarled.

"If this is just between you and me, then tell your friends to back off."

"With pleasure!" Franks spat and waved his followers away. He brandished his fist and approached Edison.

Edison punched a key on the wheelchair's console, and a

virtual grid appeared. He adjusted the grid to center Franks image. A *ping* indicated a target lock. A press of a button caused a section on either side of the hover chair's modified arms to slide back. This revealed a pair of bell-shaped muzzles which tapered into narrow snouts. The muzzles swiveled to track the bully's movement.

"Last chance!" Edison warned.

Markie hesitated, but the shouts from his gang spurred him on.

"Think your toys scare me?" he sneered and continued toward Edison.

Edison let him advance a few more feet before he tapped one last key. Suddenly, the narrow space between the two gyms filled with a simultaneous *crack* as both vortex cannons spat in unison. An ear-splitting *pop* reverberated off the walls, and Franks, arms wind-milling, was hurled backwards. He fell heavily onto the grass-covered ground adjacent to the narrow walkway. Dazed, he lay motionless for a few moments before he struggled to his feet and rubbed his bruised backside. He began to open his mouth, then jerked in surprise and froze.

His clothes were gone!

Edison gulped at the sight of Markie dressed in only his boxer shorts, hair blown back and standing straight up like straw. The bully's pants hung from a power line. His shirt, snagged on a drainpipe near the roof of the gym, flapped like a flag in the breeze. One shoe lay on the ground thirty feet away, while the other shoe was nowhere to be seen.

Markie's gang, stunned by the sudden turn of events, stared openmouthed at their leader. A deathly quiet fell until one of them, a short, stocky Hispanic kid, snorted.

"What you laughin' at, Mario?" Markie snarled.

Mario pointed and everyone noticed his boxer shorts. They

were black, and adorned with dozens of little pink pigs with heart-shaped wings.

Another snort escaped Mario's lips.

Soon, the rest of the gang pointed, and as if a dam had been breached, peals of laughter broke out.

Franks' eyes darted left and right. Like a cornered animal, he sought an avenue for escape. Humiliated, tears filled his eyes and he turned toward Edison.

His voice cracked. "I'll get you for this, Jones. If it's the last thing I do, I'll get you for this!" He turned and ran, disappearing from sight.

Silence fell once again. Markie's followers milled about, uncertain what to do in the absence of their leader. One by one, they slunk off.

Only Edison was left.

Alone, he tried to gather his thoughts. He knew he ought to feel exhilarated. He stood up to Franks and his plan worked to perfection. However, no such emotion coursed through him. Instead, he felt a sense of shame. The tears in Markie's eyes were genuine, as was his humiliation in front of his friends. It wasn't what Edison wanted.

How could I have known Markie would be wearing those ridiculous boxer shorts? I just wanted to teach him a lesson so he would leave me alone!

A heavy sigh escaped from his lips. He turned and propelled his hoverchair back toward the cafeteria. Although puzzled by how his perfect plan could have gone so wrong, he was certain of one thing.

I just made a bad situation worse.

CHAPTER 14

EDISON FIXED AN EMPTY STARE AT THE SODA IN HIS HAND, BARELY aware of the music blaring in the background.

"You blew Franks clothes off with the vortex cannon, and he was wearing little piggy boxers? *Please* tell me you videoed it so we can post it on Snapchat!" Hondo chortled and pranced a jig around Edison's hoverchair.

Edison refused to answer his friend. They were on the backyard patio at Carly's house, a large two-story affair in a new subdivision on the northeast side of town. Half a dozen dance mats faced a fifty-two inch flat-screen TV sitting atop a picnic table. The dance competition began to heat up in earnest as fellow junior high students crammed the patio, most gyrating wildly to the music.

"Dude, you're my hero!" Hondo gushed, oblivious to Edison's discomfort.

Even though Edison said nothing to anyone about the incident, word spread like wildfire among the student population. Hondo was the latest in a long line of well-wishers, many of whom had also suffered at the hands of Markie Franks and his troupe of bullies. His shoulders were so sore from congratulatory backslaps, he found himself flinching anytime someone came near.

Edison ran his hand through his hair and sighed. *The last thing I feel like is a hero.* Markie's tear-streaked face kept reappearing in his mind like an endless video loop.

Carly interrupted Edison's morose thoughts when she breezed out of a group of dancing students. "There he is!" she cried. She leaned over and gave him an energetic hug. Her skin, soft and warm, carried a faint scent of flowery perfume.

"It's about time someone stood up to Markie!" Her face flushed from dancing, Carly looked cherubic as she beamed at him

"Uh…thanks," Edison mumbled.

Someone called Carly's name. She waved at him, then turned and grabbed Hondo by the arm. In a flash, they disappeared into the throng of students. Edison stared after her, the memory of her warm cheek pressed against his fresh on his mind.

Distracted, he didn't notice Bree until she appeared at his side.

"I guess you're pretty proud of yourself." With arms crossed, she looked down at him, lips pressed in a severe line.

Startled, Edison looked up and stammered, "Well, no-not exactly."

Bree waved her hands. "You were by yourself! You could have been…you could have been hurt!"

"Well, ah, I—"

"And now that you have shown up Markie, what do you think he is going to do? Just forget about the whole thing?"

"Well, I didn't think—"

"No! You didn't think! And now he's really going to be gunning for you!" Animated, Bree bounced up and down on her toes.

Peering at her closely, Edison could see she was worried, *very* worried about him.

"What was I supposed to do, Bree? Just let Markie and his friends harass me all year?"

"No, of course not. But you could have reported him to Mr. Dirks. Or let me or your friends help you."

Edison felt his face grow warm. "Why? Because I'm in a wheelchair? Because I can't help myself?"

Bree stepped back, hand to her mouth. "You know I don't mean that."

"Really? Then tell me this. Would you have given the same advice to Hondo? How about Carly?"

Bree's silence confirmed Edison's suspicion. Angrily, he pivoted his anti-grav chair and made his way to the front door.

"Edison, stop!" Bree cried. She jumped ahead and planted herself firmly in front of his hoverchair. With the press of kids all around them, Edison couldn't continue without running into her. He cast about to find a way around her, then spied the devastated look on her face. She was so distraught, her arms and hands trembled.

Edison's anger drained away.

Bree struggled to speak. "What I mean, what I meant to say was…you don't have to sink to Markie's level. You don't have to act like him. You're a special person, Edison. I've known that from the first time I saw you—and it has nothing to do with being in a wheelchair."

Bree bent and whispered in Edison's ear, "It has everything to do with you." She brushed her lips against his cheek, then straightened and fled into the throng of twirling teens.

Edison, mouth agape, reached up and fingered his face where her lips touched. First the hug from Carly, then the butterfly kiss from Bree. He sat frozen, oblivious to everything around him, and sifted through his jumbled emotions. No test, software program, schematic, or algorithm—nothing in his life—ever challenged him like his interactions and relationships with his friends and peers.

Edison rubbed his face. A great weariness settled over him like a lead weight. Around him, everybody danced, talked, and had a good time. Everyone but him.

He pulled out his cell phone and called Carney to come pick him up.

Edison lay on a padded table in a room a short distance down the hall from his bedroom. State-of-the-art physical therapy equipment filled the area, and the air had an antiseptic quality about it.

"Why so glum?" Carney asked as he briskly rubbed down Edison's legs.

Edison took his time answering. Finally, he said, "I just have some things on my mind."

Carney arched an eyebrow. "That so?" Expertly, he manipulated Edison's legs while he continued to observe him. Finished, he scooped him up and carried him to an exercise bicycle. The ex-SEAL placed Edison in the high-backed seat. Then Carney placed each foot in specially-designed pedals, also with Velcro straps. He twisted a dial to a pre-arranged setting and the pedals turned, pumping Edison's legs. Designed to increase circulation in his limbs, it also helped prevent muscle atrophy.

Familiar with the drill, Edison held on to the handlebars as a pleasant *hum* from the electric motor filled the room. Carney, arms crossed, eyed him expectantly, and Edison knew his bodyguard was content to wait him out until he spilled what was eating at him. Desperate for someone to talk to, Edison's reluctance crumbled.

"I think I may have made a mistake at school this week."

Carney dragged a chair next to the bicycle and straddled the seat. "Okay, let's hear it."

Edison relayed his problems with Markie Franks, the repeated "collisions", and how he resolved to do something about it and stand up for himself. With a deep breath, he told Carney how he and Hondo had tested the vortex cannon, then how he lured Markie to an isolated area at school and used the cannon against him. Head bowed, he finished with what happened to Markie, and how everyone at school congratulated him and told him what a great thing he had done.

"But, I don't feel great. I feel awful," Edison whispered.

Carney blanched. "You used a weapon against a fellow student?"

"*No*! I mean yes. I mean I tested it plenty of times. There were no redundancies. I would never hurt anyone, you know that!" Edison blurted.

"Yes, I know you would never intentionally hurt anyone, but when you use experimental technology, even you, Edison, can make a mistake."

"Well, he should leave me alone! I *asked* him, I *warned* him, but he still kept coming at me."

Carney clucked his tongue. "So, let's see if I have this straight. You set a trap, baited it, and now act surprised you had to spring it?"

Edison couldn't answer. His bodyguard struck the heart of the matter. He had planned the confrontation down to the last detail, from start to finish. It had been Edison who caused the whole affair even to the point of goading Markie into following him at lunch.

Guilty as charged.

Edison pounded the top of the handlebars with his fist. "I just wanted to get him off my back. I didn't want my friends to think I couldn't take care of myself. I mean, what else was I supposed to do?"

Carney reached over and turned the speed dial off. The pedals slowly ground to a stop. He stood and leaned on the handlebars.

"Look, I understand why you did it, and I understand your frustration. It's obvious you feel badly about what happened, so I know you learned your lesson. But, you always have options, Edison, always! Think about that the next time someone pushes your button."

Carney reached over and tapped Edison's chest. "Don't let your disability influence how you think or act. Don't let it rule your emotions."

The big ex-SEAL squeezed Edison's shoulder. "I think you'll find your friends—your *true* friends—will stick with you no matter what."

Carney winked. "And that never will have anything to do with whether you were standing or sitting."

Edison felt a warmth grow inside him.

Your friends will stick with you no matter what.

His anger and hostility toward Markie Franks blinded him to this simple truth. Nevertheless, it was a valuable lesson learned.

Maybe it hadn't been such a bad week after all.

CHAPTER 15

Edison bent over and set the video sphere on top of three cylindrical rings.

He had miniaturized and improved his initial invention so each external ring represented a more powerful, stand-alone anti-grav magnet. Appearing like a trio of cheap bracelets from a dollar store, the rings rested atop the grass of the football field. Fans still streamed into the bleachers as Hondo's team and the team from Texarkana finished their warm-ups. A palpable excitement filled the cool October air, as both teams entered the fray undefeated. Hondo chattered about the game all week, and Edison knew his friend couldn't wait to play.

Edison, still puzzled how any contest, much less a seventh-grade football game, could generate such enthusiasm and emotion. There were so many things in life of much greater importance. It seemed foolish to expend so much energy and time on a game.

When he mentioned exactly that to Carney, his bodyguard laughed and proceeded to describe the facts of life to Edison about how football was viewed in Texas. He explained in many towns and cities both large and small, there were few if any events which brought out a community like football. The young and old, black, white, and Hispanic, even the rich and the poor, all showed up to stand shoulder-to-shoulder at football games.

Edison thought he understood, but then remarked at the number of people who came to the junior high football games. Surely this interest didn't extend to mere seventh-grade games!

"You've got to understand everybody likes a winner," Carney said. "And Harpersville's football program hasn't produced many winners in the past twenty years. Usually, the varsity team is always near the bottom of the district standings and never makes the play-offs. The seventh-grade team is the first team to show any promise in a long time. So, yeah, fans want to go see them."

In the larger scheme of things, it still didn't make much sense to Edison. Still, he was acutely aware of the excitement each game generated. The roar of the fans, the cheers when the team did well, the groans when they did poorly, and the electric atmosphere which existed at each and every game—all proof Carney was right.

As if to emphasize the point, the Harpersville fans cheered wildly when Hondo's team trotted to the sidelines for last minute instructions. Edison shook his head, and finished prepping the video sphere.

Anticipation rippled through Edison, and it had nothing to do with the football game. Like before, he continued to use the video sphere at the games to test his anti-grav magnet. Tonight, he was using an application which he hoped would not only solve the energy cell problem, but also allow the sphere to soar to a much higher elevation than ever before. If successful, it would open up a world of possibilities he had only dreamed about. Another shiver of excitement rippled through him, and he struggled to keep his hands from shaking while he activated the electromagnets.

Edison checked the power levels of each anti-grav ring from a digital readout on his tablet, then ran through a pre-launch checklist. Everything appeared in the green. With a deep breath, he poised his index finger just above the touch screen.

He tapped the activation key.

Nothing happened and Edison's heart sank. Then, one-by-one, the rings separated from one another, pushing the video sphere upward. Edison whooped with joy, and almost dropped his tablet in the process. He looked around afraid he caused a spectacle. He had nothing to worry about though. All eyes were on the two teams on the football field.

Quickly, Edison increased the power to each ring, gradually widening the distance between each disk. Pushed upward, the video sphere rose higher and higher.

Giddy, Edison forced himself to take a few calming breaths, then prepared to put the anti-grav rings through one more critical test. Slowly, he moved the rings horizontally. Up to this point, each disk held to a rigidly vertical line. Everything depended upon the ability of the anti-grav magnets to synchronize their movements! If even one failed to sync or produced a wobbly motion, it would set off a chain reaction…the result being the video camera would crash to the ground.

Edison continued to manipulate and test the movement of the magnets. They continued to sustain their successful synchronic movement! Realizing he was holding his breath, he exhaled.

Ten minutes later, Edison sat back, a celebration dance frolicking in his mind. The video sphere was stable and best of all, the power levels held steady.

If I can do this on a smaller scale, imagine what I can do with a much larger object!

A roar announced the kick-off, and Edison wrenched his attention back to the present. He manipulated the anti-grav magnets to position the camera and bring it closer to the action. While he panned the crowd in the visitor's bleachers to check the resolution, he spotted a familiar figure sitting alone. The boy ignored the game and looked at the video sphere. A chill ran down Edison's spine as the boy raised his hand and extended his middle finger.

Markie Franks.

After the confrontation with Edison and his vortex cannon, Markie disappeared and didn't show up at school until the end of the week. When he did, he acted like nothing had happened. He still swaggered with his gang obediently following him. Two things changed, though. First, Markie left Edison alone. There were no more "accidental" collisions. Second, Mario was exiled as a member of Markie's gang.

The day after the large bully showed back up at school, Edison spotted Mario at lunch all alone. Hunched miserably at a cafeteria table, the former member of Markie's posse sported a fat lip and a black eye, penalties administered for being the first among the gang to laugh at Markie's boxer shorts.

Since then, everyone avoided Mario like he had contracted the plague—the unspoken warning to be friendly with him was to cross Markie. Edison felt sorry for him, but inside couldn't help the sense of relief he wasn't a target anymore.

Edison returned his attention back to recording the game.

CHAPTER 16

Edison replayed the digital video, but before the last image faded, Hondo waved a slice of pizza and cried, "Show me again!" A to-go box in his other hand, Hondo leaned forward as Edison repeated yet again, the most important play of the game.

Carly, Bree, and Hondo were all gathered in Edison's room at the Jones Mansion. After a 21-14 victory over Texarkana on Thursday—a historic win since no Harpersville football team had beaten Texarkana in years, Hondo had described for Carly and Bree the high definition panels which made up Edison's walls, and their spectacular Imax-like effect. The next thing Edison knew, Carly and Bree had called their parents to ask permission to go to the mansion and see for themselves.

Edison nodded, and skipped the digital footage ahead with the game tied at 14, and a little over four minutes left in the game. With Harpersville on their own 30-yard line, Hondo faked a hand-off and dropped back for a pass. The Texarkana defensive linemen didn't bite on the play fake, and moments later, Hondo was scrambling for his life. Chased out of the pocket, he raced past the line of scrimmage, stiff-armed a would-be tackler, and burst down the field. With defenders in hot pursuit, Hondo bobbed and weaved until the last Texarkana player met him at the 10-yard line. Hit with bruising impact, Hondo refused to go down and muscled his way into the end zone carrying the tackler with him.

Touchdown!

Carly and Bree cheered and clapped. The clarity of the video was so lifelike, it made it appear like they were still at the game. Even Edison found himself caught up in the excitement. The end of the replay showed Hondo spiking the ball and mobbed by happy teammates.

Carly performed an impromptu backflip, then hugged Hondo. At the sight of Carly's embrace of his big friend, jealousy mushroomed inside Edison, and he gripped the arms of the hoverchair.

As quickly as it filled him, it disappeared.

Hondo blurted, "Hey, Edison, why don't you show Carly and Bree your secret lab!"

Both girls turned toward Edison. Caught off guard, Edison mumbled, "Huh? My secret lab?"

Any further hesitation evaporated when Carly, her face animated, said, "You have a secret lab? Can we see it? Please!"

"Sure." He moved the hoverchair to the wall and placed his hand on the scanner. Moments later, two panels whispered apart where once a seamless facade existed. Edison grinned at the girls' reaction to the sight of the pneumatic elevator. Mouths agape, they stood rooted in place while Edison and Hondo entered the elevator car.

"Well, whatcha waiting for?" Hondo drawled.

Carly and Bree looked at one another, giggled, and jumped in. Once inside, Edison punched keys on the control panel, and two additional seats dropped soundlessly from a recess in the walls.

Hondo took charge like a tour guide, and smugly showed both girls how to pull out their seatbelts and attach them. Then he sat back, arms crossed, and grinned in anticipation.

Once everyone was securely seated, Edison spoke, "Level twenty," and the pneumatic car began to move. With a faintly audible *whisk*, the elevator traveled a short distance, then dropped in a stomach-clenching plummet. Carly and Bree screamed, Hondo's howls of laughter joining them.

"Sorry," Edison apologized. "We'll be there in just a minute."

Eyes wide, both girls clenched the sides of their seats. Carly recovered first. A smile flitted across her face, and she released her death grip on the seat. She raised her arms over her head like she was on a rollercoaster, and cried, "Whee!"

Bree kept her firm grip, however, the look of fear fading to one of relief when the car finally slowed to a stop.

The elevator doors *hissed* open. Hondo jumped out of his seat and stood at the opening with a huge grin. He motioned to Carly and Bree. "Isn't that a rush?"

Both girls unbuckled their seatbelts and stumbled out. Edison shot Hondo a venomous look, and in return, Hondo's grin got even wider. "Hey, you didn't warn me about your rollercoaster ride either!"

Carly and Bree looked around, their reaction much like Hondo's on his first trip to the underground lab. As Edison led the group of friends deeper into his workroom, motion-activated banks of lights flickered on. At Hondo's urging, Edison told the girls the history of the underground facilities. Dutifully, Edison related what he told Hondo and repeated the showing of the video montage of the facilities' construction.

Impatient with Edison's pace, Hondo finally blurted "We're twenty stories beneath the ground!"

Bree shook her head. "So this whole lab complex…it's buried way beneath the earth?"

"Yep!" Hondo answered for Edison. "That's why no one can spy on Edison and his grandfather's company or steal the stuff they invent either."

Carly and Bree, palms to their cheeks, gawked as they continued their trek through the lab. Hondo's eyes widened and he pointed to a corner of the lab. "Hey, what's that?"

Edison grinned. "C'mon, I'll show you." The anti-grav chair shot forward, and Hondo, Carly, and Bree had to jog to catch up with him.

Three large pallets rested on motorized platforms. Two contained five, large cylindrical rings stacked one on top of the other. Each disk, approximately ten feet in diameter, consisted of a copper-hued metallic construction. Smooth and featureless except for three blister-like protrusions, the "blisters" were arranged on each ring at points exactly equidistant from each other.

On the third pallet rested a single ring thicker and smaller in diameter than the others. A blunt, egg-shaped module—twenty feet in height—rose from this ring. The pod was attached to the ring by multiple struts much like spokes on a wheel. The outline of an oval door appeared on the side of the module with *Journey I* stenciled over it. Next to the door was a narrow observation window constructed of thick glass. Except for the black letters on *Journey I*, the pod was painted a brilliant white.

Hondo scratched his head. "What is all this? What are those things?"

Carly and Bree, eyes locked on the pallets, nodded in agreement.

With a wide grin, Edison gestured at the rings. "This represents what I hope is the future of space exploration. It will revolutionize launch technology and how payloads are delivered into outer space. Everything from satellites to space stations will be affected by it."

Edison's friends stared at him like he just spoke in a foreign language. Exasperated, he sped his hoverchair to a nearby workbench. There he picked up several objects which looked like miniature copies of the giant rings. He placed them on the floor, backed up, and turned his attention to a control console.

"Enable," Edison commanded, then turned to his friends. "The largest rocket ever built was the *Saturn V* produced for the Apollo Space program. Designed to allow NASA to put a man on the moon, the *Saturn V* rocket had a mass of three thousand metric tons. That's six million six hundred and ninety-nine thousand pounds. When placed upright in launch mode, the Saturn V rocket stood three hundred and sixty-three feet high, or fifty-eight feet taller than the Statue of Liberty. Despite the massive size of the rocket, its payload capacity was only around one hundred thousand pounds."

Edison tapped the touchscreen on his tablet. His friends gasped as the rings rose from the floor, separated, and hovered motionless before them.

"The Saturn V was enormously expensive to produce, and NASA retired the rocket at the conclusion of the Apollo program. The Space Shuttle became the primary launch vehicle for NASA, but the Shuttle's payload capacity—twenty-eight thousand kilograms—represents only twenty-five percent of the payload of the Saturn V rocket. The European Space Agency's launch vehicle, the Ariane 5, has a payload capacity of sixteen thousand kilograms, which is even less."

Edison laid the controller in his lap. "So, as you can see, payload capacity for any current rocket or launch vehicle is extremely limited."

Silence greeted his explanation. Hondo said, "Uh...Edison? You remember our little talk when we were in the clearing with Bob the Mannequin? About how we are just kids and that you need to talk in English?"

"Huh?" Edison cleared his throat. "Oh. Yes."

Edison took a deep breath. "Launching anything into outer

space is expensive, whether it is satellites, space probes, or even parts to the International Space Station. What's more, there are definite limitations to how large the mass of the payload can be—"

"English!"

"Ah, that is, the bigger or heavier the object, the harder it is to launch it into geostationary or geosynchronous orbit—"

"Kids here!"

"Yes, I mean the harder it is to place an object in a stable orbit stationary to ground controllers or observers back here on earth."

The words tumbled from Edison's mouth in a rush. "You see, these anti-gravity rings create what in essence is a space elevator. It solves the problem of breaking free of earth's gravity and placing objects in outer space regardless of size and mass."

"Space elevator? You mean like an elevator in a building that goes up and down?" Bree asked.

"Yes!" Edison blurted. "Look, the concept of a space elevator isn't even new. A Russian scientist, Konstantin Tsiolkovsky, first proposed this theory in 1895. While much of the science behind Tsiolkovsky's space elevator proposal is more comic book than hard science, several well respected aerospace engineers and researchers have incorporated some of Tsiolkovsky's key concepts into their own theoretical space elevators."

"Oh no," Hondo groaned. "Why do I feel like we're back in Mr. Russell's class at school? Can't you give a simple explanation just once, Edison?"

"Hondo, you're hopeless," Bree said with a shake of her head. She looped her arm with Carly's. "We want to hear more."

Despite the sour look on his big friend's face, Edison eagerly continued, "Some theoretical researchers have proposed a space elevator could be produced by constructing a tether. The tether, like a rope, would be anchored from somewhere along the earth's equatorial region and stretch into geostationary orbit. The tether would then be used to transport objects into space...just like Tsiolkovsky envisioned!"

"Then why ain't it been done?" Hondo asked.

"All sorts of reasons," Edison replied. "The enormous cost for one, technological limitations for another. There have been some breakthroughs with carbon nanotube technology from which the tether could be constructed—"

"Still kids here!"

"Huh? Oh, yes. Uh, what I mean is that cost and current technology make construction of a tethered space elevator impossible at this time."

Edison cleared his throat. "Power down," he ordered, and the rings drifted back to the floor. He motioned to Hondo. "See that round, metal ball on my work table?"

Hondo nodded.

"Can you bring it over here?"

Hondo walked to the table. A grunt escaped from his lips when he picked up the heavy metal ball. He carried it over to Edison. "Hey, this is a shot put! Where did you get it?"

"I asked Coach Macklin if I could borrow it for an experiment. Anyway, can you place it on top of the first ring, please?"

Edison manipulated the controller and caused the first two rings to rise and separate, leaving only the first ring on the floor. Gingerly, Hondo took the heavy shot and placed it on top of the disk. Wiping his hands on his jeans, he stepped away.

Edison returned his attention to the controls and input a series of commands. Slowly, the iron sphere wobbled and rose from the ring. Lips pursed in concentration, he quickly made adjustments and the oscillating stopped.

Next, the ring rose from the floor, raising the shot as it did so. It stopped three feet above the ground. Edison turned to the pair of anti-gravity rings hovering nearby. He tapped the touchscreen and moved one of the cylindrical disks toward the metal ball. The disk inserted itself directly beneath the shot put, followed by the last remaining ring. All three disks were now aligned beneath the heavy ball. The wobble became more pronounced.

"Look out!" Hondo cried, certain the shot put was going to fall.

Undeterred, Edison concentrated fiercely, determined to reestablish the equilibrium of the anti-gravity rings. The controls became a battleground, commands sent, amended, then adjusted yet again as Edison struggled to sync the anti-grav disks. Just when it seemed the heavy object would tumble to the ground, the oscillations stopped, and the shot put rose several feet above the rings.

Hondo cheered and hooted while Carly and Bree clapped. Additional manipulations by Edison caused the anti-gravity rings to rise higher and lower, then horizontally across the floor. Perched above the topmost anti-gravity disk like a bobbing cork, the shot moved in unison with the circular disks. Finally, Edison lowered the anti-gravity rings one-by-one to the floor, the metal ball resting on top.

He powered down the disks and turned to his friends, a satisfied grin on his face. "Well, what do you think?"

Bree, the first to speak, said, "Edison, it's fantastic! What's next?"

Edison's grin grew even wider. "Glad you asked that, because you're all invited!"

Puzzled, Hondo asked, "To what?"

"To the first large-scale test of my AGMAG." Edison gestured toward the pallets. "On Saturday, we're going to activate those anti-gravity rings and test the space elevator."

He maneuvered his hoverchair forward and stopped by

the oval pod. Running his hand over the smooth metal surface, Edison's gaze lingered for just a moment before he turned to his friends.

"You see, I'm going to launch this module into orbit."

And then bring it back down."

CHAPTER 17

FRIDAY DRAGGED BY WITH GLACIAL SLOWNESS.

Edison repeatedly checked his cell for the time. It didn't help that Hondo, Carly, and Bree peppered him with questions throughout the day about the upcoming test of the space elevator. His phone vibrated continuously with text after text from them. They seemed more excited than he was.

Edison also found it hard to keep his attention on school. In his math class, the teacher had to call upon him *twice* to answer a question. Then he forgot to turn in an assignment for history and had to be reminded by Bree.

His mind continued to focus on the mental checklist prepared for the launch of the space module. There were a million and one details to consider, and although confident of success, Edison knew it only took one glitch, one overlooked detail, to cause the entire test to fail.

Mercifully, the school day finally ended. Although he wanted to rush home, crunch numbers, and go over every aspect of tomorrow's launch, Edison promised Hondo that Carney would drive them to the varsity football game in Longview. Afterward, Hondo planned to spend the night, while Bree and Carly would meet them at the Jones Mansion early Saturday morning.

Edison propelled his anti-grav chair out of the school

building. He made a turn to the parent pick-up area where Carney waited for both of them. One thought kept percolating through his mind.

Tomorrow can't come fast enough!

Edison tossed and turned. He couldn't sleep. His mind kept drifting to the launch. The sounds from Hondo's bed indicated he had trouble sleeping too, although Edison wasn't sure if it was the test launch or the 40-0 drubbing the varsity football team took which kept him awake.

The entire drive home, Carney and Hondo engaged in a lively discussion over football schemes and tactics. Edison, his thoughts a million miles away, could only think of the space elevator test. They arrived home late, and both boys went immediately to bed.

Flat on his back, Edison stared at the ceiling. Suddenly, Hondo's voice pierced the darkness.

"Can't sleep either, huh?"

Startled, Edison replied, "Uh, no. I can't stop thinking about the launch."

"Hey, don't worry about it. My money's on you. Besides, even if something goes wrong, you'll get it fixed."

Edison wished he could be as certain of success as Hondo. Before he could process the thought further, Hondo spoke again.

"You know, we got our butts kicked tonight. It ticked me off, and I got all freaked out, but you know what? Even if we had won, it wouldn't have changed anything."

Edison, uncertain where Hondo was going with this, turned his head and tried to see his friend in the murky darkness.

"What do you mean?"

"I mean what you're doing tomorrow is important—something that will last. Years from now, no one will remember Harpersville lost a football game. They *will* remember Edison Jones invented a space elevator."

The unexpected comment left Edison speechless. He didn't know what to say. Then Hondo dropped another bombshell.

"You know, sometimes…sometimes I wish I could be like you." Hondo flipped on his side and concluded the conversation. Moments later, Hondo's deep even breaths indicated he had fallen asleep.

Edison couldn't believe his ears. *Hondo wants to be like me? Everybody cheers for him, and I can't even stand much less run.*

How many times did he secretly wish he had been the one running down the field for a touchdown instead of Hondo? How many times did he wish Carly would look at him just once, the way she always looked at Hondo?

His thoughts and emotions, tossed to and fro within the tempest of his mind, would give him no rest. No matter how hard he tried, he couldn't reconcile his feelings with the deep streak of logic ingrained within him. A part of him contained an insatiable curiosity—one which wanted to push the envelope of science and technology to the limit and beyond.

Another part just wanted to run and catch a football.

Weariness overtook him, and turning, he fell into a deep, dreamless sleep.

"This is so exciting!" Carly bubbled.

Carly, Bree, and Hondo stood once again in Edison's underground lab. The girls' parents had dropped them off earlier that morning. Their eagerness to witness the test launch rivaled even Edison's.

An audible *hum* came from the motorized pallets loaded with the anti-gravity rings and space module. Edison, busy using a remote controller to maneuver the pallets, was too occupied to spare Carly a glance. Couplings protruded from each pallet, and Edison attached each one like box cars on a train. Then, he slid from his wheelchair and into an oversized golf cart, the anti-grav chair folding itself into a storage trunk in the back. Edison backed the cart up and after some maneuvering, managed to attach it to the coupling on the lead pallet.

"C'mon!" Edison called to his friends.

They piled into the cart. Hondo took shotgun next to Edison with the girls sitting behind them. Edison nudged the throttle control lever on the dash and the cart began to move with the pallets snaking behind. They headed toward a solid wall, and Edison grinned when his friends gasped at the eminent collision. Without slowing down, he pressed a button inset on the cart's steering wheel.

With a barely audible whisper, the entire section of the wall slid upward!

Hondo whooped and released his grip on the seat as they rumbled through the opening. Squeaks of relief came from Bree and Carly. Bree slapped Edison on his shoulder.

"You know, you could warn us next time!" she scolded.

Laughing, Edison steered the little convoy down a broad corridor. Brightly lit, the wide passage allowed several of the vehicles to pass by one another with room to spare. Spaced at regular intervals on the ceiling, LED lighting glinted off reflective, neon yellow stripes. Painted onto the smooth, gray concrete floor, the stripes divided the pathway into equal halves. As they trundled along, other corridors appeared to form intersections. Periodically, large letter and number combinations appeared stenciled on the otherwise featureless concrete walls.

Hondo pointed at the block-print letter and number combinations. "What are those for?"

"Oh. That stands for 'Echo-Two' or the section of the facility we're traveling through," Edison replied. "The underground complex is enormous, and each section is connected by means of these passageways. Letters and numbers are assigned to the different lab and research modules and the corridor which connects them. It's too easy to get lost otherwise."

Moments later, the cart and its train of pallets turned a corner and merged into a much larger thoroughfare. More of a road than a corridor, other traffic soon joined them. All of the LogicTech vehicles seemed to be going in the same direction, and Edison got in line behind a small flatbed truck. Shortly, they came across intersections with traffic lights mounted on struts bolted to the ceiling. Edison brought the convoy to a stop at a red light. Vehicle traffic surged by through adjacent passages.

"Wow. An underground rush hour," Hondo quipped.

Soon they were on the move again, and after traveling less than five minutes, the line of vehicles halted yet again. Edison pointed to a security checkpoint, and his friends craned their necks to get a better view. Stubby, solid steel poles sheathed in molded bright red plastic, protruded from the floor to provide a barrier to traffic. A guard stood checking the credentials of every vehicle which passed by. Each driver gave the guard a plastic card which he swiped across a small monitor.

At Hondo's puzzled expression, Edison explained, "It's an electronic eye. Each employee of LogicTech is issued a card with a memory chip embedded in it. The chip contains all the employee's information such as their name, the shift they're working, and their job description. No one can move past any of the checkpoints without their card."

A high-pitched beep emanated from the security checkpoint,

and the steel posts of the barrier sank into the floor. When the vehicle passed by, a warning klaxon sounded, and the barrier rose again. The friends waited as the guard quickly and efficiently processed each vehicle. Soon, it was their turn and Edison handed over his own card.

The light blue sleeve of the guard's uniform inched up his arm and his sidearm jiggled at his hip as he greeted them with a friendly wave. "Good morning, Mr. Jones."

Edison glanced at the LogicTech security badge to remind him of the guard's name. "Good morning, Carlos," Edison replied.

Carlos scanned the card, then returned it. "Heard there's big doings topside. The whole facility is buzzing about it. Good luck, sir!" A beep sounded and the barrier lowered.

Edison grinned. "Thanks, Carlos."

Nudging the cart forward, the train of pallets rumbled by and soon they were on their way again. After negotiating several more twists and turns, Edison could tell from his friend's faces they had completely lost their bearings and sense of direction.

Edison smiled and pointed at a screen on the cart's dashboard. It displayed a grid of the underground facility. "Even with our letter and number system, veteran employees can get lost. So just in case, everyone within the research annex has GPS."

They turned at another intersection and rounded the corner. A large platform appeared at the end of the thoroughfare. Two, snub-nosed, cargo trucks were already parked on it, with a third in the process of driving onto the flat surface. Without hesitation, Edison drove the cart and train of pallets onto the platform.

At his friends' questioning looks, Edison explained, "This is a freight elevator. It will take us to the surface." Edison's pulse began to quicken.

It won't be long now!

CHAPTER 18

A SHARP CHIRP PIERCED THE AIR, AND THE FREIGHT ELEVATOR'S doors slid shut.

Moments later, the floor shivered and they began to rise. A digital screen inset on the elevator's panel flashed the decreasing number of levels of the underground facility. The lift slowed to a stop, and a pleasant feminine voice chirped, "Ground level A". The doors slid open and bright sunlight streamed in.

Edison waited until the other cargo trucks exited the elevator before he drove off with his little convoy. He blinked in the brilliant morning light, his friends observing the beehive of activity with mouths agape.

A huge pad of concrete was located a short distance away from the cargo elevator. Numerous trucks and cars were parked on the cement apron, all bearing the "LogicTech" logo. A gigantic transmission tower, one hundred meters tall, stretched skyward from the tarmac, a squat, windowless cinderblock building at its base. Instrumentation sprouted from the roof of the building in an odd profusion of antenna and dish components. A dozen technicians swarmed about, some checking equipment and others loading cargo. A phalanx of LogicTech security guards overlooked the entire operation.

Edison's appearance galvanized the LogicTech staff into more frenetic activity. As he directed the cart down a recently paved roadway, one LogicTech security car pulled in front while another fell in behind. The blacktop snaked through a dense grove of trees and disappeared from sight. Edison pushed the cart's speed to high, and pulled onto the asphalt ribbon to follow the lead security car. Other LogicTech vehicles soon followed, and the air filled with the rumble of their movement.

The cool autumn air rushed by making conversation almost impossible. A young forest, a mixture of pines and hardwood trees interspersed here and there with ponds, small lakes, and pastures, flashed by.

Bree tapped him on the shoulder and shouted, "It's so beautiful. Is this whole area reclaimed land?"

Edison nodded. "The entire region for miles and miles at one time was strip-mined," he shouted back.

They traveled over a mile when another clearing suddenly appeared. Here, a second group of LogicTech employees and vehicles awaited them. Another enormous concrete pad had been poured, but this one contained an odd set of concentric rings inset into the tarmac. Like rails on a railroad track, they curved to form a loop. Flush with the flat surface, they emanated outward from smaller circles to larger.

A control tower adjacent to the tarmac thrust high into the air. As Edison brought the cargo cart to a stop, a familiar figure emerged from the tower and trotted over to them.

"What took you so long?" Carney asked with a wink.

"Traffic was kinda heavy," Edison replied with a huge grin. "Is everything ready?"

"Just waiting for you."

Carney welcomed Hondo and the girls, then led them to the tower. LogicTech scientists and technicians swarmed over the pallets and moved them to the center of the pad. There they assembled the anti-gravity rings around the module.

Once inside the control tower, a small elevator took them to the top where Stanton Jones met them. A twinkle in his eye, he said, "It's your baby from here on out, Edison. If this test launch is successful, your anti-gravity elevator will be a prototype which changes forever how payloads are delivered into space. It might even revive space exploration."

Jones placed a hand on Edison's shoulder. "Regardless of what happens, I'm proud of you."

"Thanks, Grandpa. I'll do my best," Edison promised.

"Hey, it'll be all right, Mr. Jones. Edison's got this covered!" Hondo chimed.

Bree moved closer. "I'm proud, I mean we're proud of you too." Her face red from the verbal slip, Bree quickly turned away.

A voice crackled from the speakers. *"Launch control. All components assembled. Do we have a go to activate the antigravity rings?"*

Everyone looked at Edison.

With a deep breath, Edison powered the hoverchair to a bank of instruments beneath the control tower windows. The console curved in a horseshoe-shape to follow the contour of the interior walls. A half-dozen LogicTech technicians stood at their stations—all with their eyes on Edison.

Edison grabbed a pair of wireless headphones from the control panel, and placed them on his head. He adjusted the lip mike, then flashed a thumbs up to his Grandpa, Carney, and his friends.

"Ground, this is control. You have a go!"

"Roger that. We are green for go, repeat green for go!"

Edison's excitement mounted. The monitors above the control console displayed a digital countdown.

In less than five minutes, my space elevator will be launched!

A figure detached itself from within the crowded interior of the control tower and stopped beside Edison.

"Let me be the first to wish you the best of luck."

EDISON JONES AND THE ANTI-GRAV ELEVATOR

The man extended a hand to Edison. Of medium build, he had dark, silver-tipped hair swept back like wings on his head. His dark eyes peered at Edison from a tanned, clean-shaven face, and he wore an expensive pin-striped suit complete with a silk tie. The man's voice dripped with condescension, and Edison took an immediate dislike to him.

Stanton Jones' voice cut through his thoughts. "Edison, this is Cutter Gentry from NASA. He is here as an official observer. As you might expect, NASA is *very* interested in the results of the space elevator launch."

Edison reached up and gripped Gentry's hand. It had a dry, raspy, reptilian feel about it, and he fought the overwhelming urge to jerk his hand away. Instead he managed, "Pleased to meet you."

"Yes, we at NASA are always interested in any new developments involving launch technology, particularly payload capacity. From what your grandfather has told me, your space elevator looks promising."

Cynicism oozed from the statement, as if Gentry had weighed and passed judgment already on the whole project. Although he tried to mask it, it was also clear to Edison that Gentry felt the entire endeavor a waste of his time.

"The best minds in the field have been unable to solve the payload problem. It's always too much time, too much expense. Nothing so far has been economically feasible. But if you, a twelve-year old boy, can provide a solution," a Cheshire-like smile appeared on the NASA observer's face, "then we will forever be in your debt."

Edison's distaste of the man deepened.

A loud *beep* stopped all conversation, and everyone turned to the digital display.

The countdown began.

CHAPTER 19

THE CONTROL ROOM EXPLODED INTO ACTIVITY.

Gentry forgotten, Edison concentrated on the console's data stream. Although the mission computer would control the actual launch, Edison was poised to take over in an instant if adjustments were needed.

Tinted windows completely encircled the observation deck of the control tower. The throng—including Hondo, Bree, and Carly—crowded next to the windows to await the launch of the space elevator; all except for Gentry who hung back and studied his nails rather than jockey for a position.

Caught up in the excitement of the impending launch, this went unnoticed by everyone in the room except Edison. Then he saw Carney regarding the NASA official with a hard-eyed look. The ex-SEAL nodded to himself, then made his way to the observation window to join the others.

"So how's this work, anyway?" Hondo asked, squeezing next to Edison, eyes glued to the tarmac.

Edison ripped his attention back to the countdown. He studied the data scrolling across the monitor and said, "Those rails you see set into the launch pad are actually anti-gravity coils. They form the floor which the antigravity rings push off of. There are ten coils, nine of which will be used to escape the first four layers of the earth's atmosphere. The tenth ring will be used for the exosphere."

Hondo grimaced. "The what-o-sphere?"

Bree chimed in. "The exosphere is the fifth and last layer of the earth's atmosphere. If you listened in science class, you'd know. We went over this just last week."

Hondo huffed, "How was I supposed to know I would actually need to know this stuff?" Bree shook her head and turned back to the launch pad.

Edison chuckled, then clicked a few keys. A schematic of the atmosphere appeared on the screens above the control console. Each layer was represented by a separate color.

"Here you see a display of all five layers of the earth's atmosphere."

Hondo moaned. "Now look what you've done, Bree. We're not even at school and I'm going to be taught a lesson!"

Carney chuckled, and even Stanton Jones couldn't hide a smile. Carney's laughter pierced the tense atmosphere of the control room, and other LogicTech employees joined in. Only Gentry appeared unamused.

With an eye on the digital countdown, Edison said, "It will have to be a fast lesson, Hondo!" He highlighted the first layer of the atmosphere.

"This is the troposphere, the thickest layer of the atmosphere where most weather takes place. The troposphere extends from about thirty thousand feet at the poles, to about fifty-six thousand feet at the equator."

Hondo smirked at Bree. "Yeah. I think I remember that."

Edison continued. "The next layer is the stratosphere and it is approximately thirty-two miles thick. Many pilots like to use the stratosphere to fly in because the atmosphere is thinner with less air turbulence."

The young scientist highlighted the third stratum. "Next is the mesosphere, and its thickness ranges from fifty to fifty-five miles. This is where most meteors burn up. If you have ever seen a meteor shower, the streaks of light are the vaporization of the meteor within the mesosphere.

"The thermosphere is the fourth layer and here, temperatures rise rapidly up to two thousand seven hundred degrees Fahrenheit. Its thickness varies from two hundred and twenty miles to five hundred miles. The International Space Station is located within the thermosphere."

Edison pointed at the final tier on the monitor. "The last layer is called the exosphere, and can extend outward to ten thousand kilometers. Here, molecules of gas are so widely dispersed, where the exosphere ends and the vacuum of outer space begins is not well defined."

Edison turned. "What I am hoping to do today is place *Journey I* in the lower reaches of the exosphere, then bring her back down again safely."

Edison found it hard to contain his excitement. "If we can do that, then it should be possible to place any object or payload in a stable, geostationary orbit!"

He stroked a key to display the interior view of the module on the monitors. It revealed a mannequin strapped to a heavily padded chair.

Hondo's eyes widened. "Is that who I think it is?" When Edison nodded sheepishly, Hondo crowed, "Bob and *Journey I*! An unbeatable combination! Looks like you finally found Bob's clothes—"

Hondo clapped his hand to his mouth when he realized what he was saying. The others in the room looked at Hondo curiously, clueless. Carney, however, had already connected the dots, an amused look on his face.

Edison cheeks warmed and he quickly resumed his narrative. "Ah, uh, yes. As you can see, a mannequin is part of the launch of the space elevator. Bob is embedded with sensors to simulate the human body. The space pod is constructed to maintain viable living conditions throughout the period of the launch. In the early days of rocketry, lab animals were sent into space to test atmospheric integrity. With today's technology, it is possible to simulate everything from oxygen levels within the module, to the stress placed upon the various organs of the human body. Bob is our guinea pig and will continuously stream data."

With that, Edison caused another monitor to display a digital heartbeat. *Beep, beep, beep*, went the monitor.

Hondo laughed. "So, Bob has a heart after all!"

A soft chime chirped within the control room followed by a synthesized female voice. *"One minute to launch, repeat, one minute to launch."*

Everyone's attention riveted to the launch pad where the anti-gravity rings were activated. One by one, the disks rose into the air.

The rings stopped rising thirty feet above the pad. The crowd within the tower watched breathlessly as the first ring detached from the other disks. It slid to a position centered above the anti-gravity coils. Each ring, one-by-one, took a position above the disk below it. Finally, only the space module, *Journey I*, remained.

"The anti-gravity coils provide the base which the first ring pushes against," Edison explained. "Then each successive anti-gravity ring pushes against the one below it. As each disk engages, it rises above the one underneath it. Because gravity weakens the further from the earth's surface each ring is pushed, those closest to the earth are spaced more narrowly where gravity is strongest, while the outermost disks are spaced much farther apart. The tenth and last ring will actually be in the exosphere."

"The tricky part," Edison continued, "is the module itself. You'll see that it looks as if it is attached to an anti-gravity ring. However, it is actually a much smaller version of the anti-gravity coils like those embedded in the launch pad."

Carly spoke for the first time. "Why?"

A voice shot from the back of the room. "Because you need a way to return to earth." Heads swiveled to the back of the control tower in search of the speaker. Cutter Gentry stood, arms folded, his disinterested look gone. In its place was a cold and calculating expression.

"Without a way to reverse the polarity of the anti-gravity coils, once the space pod reaches zero gravity, it would continue to push away from earth. From there, it would drift in space, lost forever."

The NASA observer made his way toward the observation windows he earlier deigned to ignore. "An even worse scenario could occur if the module was placed in an unstable, decaying orbit. Then, at some point, it would reenter earth's atmosphere and burn up…at least we *hope* it would, since surviving reentry means it could possibly strike a populated area."

Gentry smirked. "Am I correct, Edison?"

Edison swallowed. "Yes."

"Hence you can see why NASA has concerns beyond simply launching your space elevator. It must also conform to standards of safety we can support."

"Spoken like a true government bureaucrat," Stanton Jones remarked. "And I'm sure you are aware that LogicTech shares your concerns for safety. Redundancies have been built into the launch system for just such contingencies. I've had my engineers go over all the schematics detail-by-detail."

Jones winked at Edison, then turned back toward Gentry. "And they report they can find no flaws in the space elevator's design."

Gentry inclined his head. In a saccharine-laced voice, he said, "I expected no less from a company with LogicTech's impressive record of success."

The synthesized voice rang out within the room as it commenced the verbal countdown, and Edison's attention was wrenched back to the anti-gravity rings.

"*10…9…8…7…6*"

Only seconds remained to launch!

CHAPTER 20

Quickly, Edison linked the modem with an exterior visual displayed on the monitors. It showed the rings arrayed above the launch pad. As the countdown reached zero a hush fell over the control room.

"Beginning launch sequence," the pleasant feminine voice intoned.

Journey I slowly rose from the tarmac. Edison directed the interior view of the module to be exhibited on several of the screens. Bob sat strapped in his seat, his mannequin face permanently frozen into a smile.

With a mischievous grin, Edison manipulated a joystick on a handheld controller. Bob's head turned to look straight at the camera. Then, his left arm raised and waved.

"Look! Bob's waving at us," Hondo cried.

Jaws dropped at the sight of Bob moving as if come to life, followed by a noisy babble as everyone tried to talk at once.

Edison called out. "Relax everybody. I had a little extra time, so I installed servo motors in Bob." The excited chatter dissolved into laughter.

Stifling a chuckle, Stanton Jones managed to ask, "Edison, don't you think you have more important things to attend to?"

"Sorry, Grandpa. Just got one more thing to do." Using the joystick, Edison caused Bob's hand to turn.

To a thumbs up.

Cheers erupted and even Gentry joined in with a few half-hearted claps.

Edison turned. *"Now* we're ready, Grandpa!"

Edison returned his complete attention to *Journey I*. The space pod continued to rise until it maneuvered above the tenth and last disk. Holding his breath, Edison waited for the final and most difficult procedure to take place. Since the module had its own anti-gravity coil, it would have to slide over and above the last anti-grav ring, while simultaneously syncing the polarity of the coil with the disk. It was a delicate process made possible only by the powerful LogicTech computer controlling the operation. The maneuvering had to be flawless, or the space pod would wobble, become unbalanced, and fall back to earth.

Edison was determined that would not happen.

Slowly but surely, *Journey I* moved into position. All eyes were glued to the module until it finally settled above the ring.

Journey I never wavered throughout the entire process.

The control room exploded a second time into wild cheers. Pumping a fist above his head, a cry of triumph erupted from Edison.

Events then proceeded rapidly with the first antigravity disk rising steadily, pushing the other rings and the space pod upward until they were lost from sight. Edison switched to exterior cameras on *Journey I*, and the monitors streamed live video images.

From the bird's eye view of the space pod, the ground shrank away until it became a checkerboard panorama of fields and pastures with the glittering blue here and there of a pond or lake. Rivers and streams appeared as snakelike coils that meandered across the land in sweeping curves. The video feed was temporarily obscured by wispy clouds…then suddenly they were above the clouds!

A chirp issued from the monitors and the synthesized female voice stated, *"First stage complete."*

Edison maneuvered the module's cameras to display the first anti-gravity ring. Now stationary, it began to recede from sight as the space pod, pushed by the second ring, continued to rise away from the earth's surface.

For the first time, the curvature of the earth appeared on *Journey I's* video stream. Land masses and oceans became defined, and the mighty Mississippi River appeared as a bright ribbon of blue stretching across the North American continent. The swirling pinwheel of a storm system perched over the northwestern part of the United States.

Edison's friends watched, transfixed, at the earth's dwindling sphere. No one spoke. The control room remained silent except for the periodic chirp announcing each stage and position of the anti-gravity rings. The atmosphere had thinned to the point where it was now tinged with a darkening hue, the earth displayed in a brilliant ball of cobalt blue against the void of space.

"It's beautiful," Bree whispered. Hondo and Carly nodded, their eyes glued to the video screens.

A warning klaxon broke the silence. Edison and the technicians scrambled to return their attention back to the instruments and closely monitor the anti-gravity elevator's progress. The most crucial stage was about to begin.

"Initiating final phase of stage separation," the computer-generated voice intoned.

With intense concentration, Edison studied the data scrolling across his monitor. He waved at his friends. "Nothing to worry about. It just means the space pod takes it from here. The computer will bring *Journey I's* anti-gravity coils to full power, and she will provide the push to bring her into geostationary position."

"Yes, one *hopes* it will be a successful endeavor." Gentry

remarked. With arms crossed, he took a position across from the technicians and monitors where he could view both closely.

Edison gulped. So far the first test of the anti-gravity elevator had gone flawlessly. However, the NASA observer was right about this last and final stage of the test. The inability to successfully place *Journey* I in proper orbit and then bring her back to earth would mean a failed test. It would be nothing more than an expensive exercise on par with a model rocket launch.

Edison stole a look at Gentry. From the NASA official's smug expression, Gentry fully expected the final stage to be unsuccessful. A cold determination grew within Edison. *I will not fail!* With great difficulty, Edison placed his feelings aside and returned his attention to the instruments.

Time for Journey I to make history!

With the tenth and last anti-grav disk in stationary position, the video feed displayed the ring rapidly shrinking as the module's anti-gravity coil pushed away. With the blue ball of the earth in the background, the darkness of space enveloped *Journey I*. The inky blackness was total, a cold, sterile darkness which seemed to lower the temperature within the control room a few degrees.

Edison paused. "Because gravity is so weak at this point, the energy required to negate and overcome it is just a fraction of what's needed at the earth's surface. That's why *Journey I*'s anti-gravity coil can actually push her farther into outer space than all the rest of the anti-grav disks combined."

Edison caused a color graphic to appear on a large monitor. It displayed an image of the earth with a tiny, blinking caricature of the module to mark from where the launch of the space elevator originated. A green line, graduated into kilometers and miles, rose from the launch site to show the trajectory of the space elevator. The line terminated in outer space as a pulsing red mark.

Edison pointed at the winking dot. "Our target placement of *Journey I* is two hundred and eighty miles. This is the orbital range of many satellites, which includes the International Space Station. Once there, we'll begin the process of bringing *Journey I* back to earth."

The last ring had long since been swallowed up in the stygian darkness and disappeared from sight. There was nothing more to see other than the slowly receding brilliant blue sphere of the earth.

It now became a waiting game.

CHAPTER 21

EDISON'S EYES LOCKED ON THE DATA SCROLLING ACROSS THE SCREEN. So far the space elevator had performed flawlessly. *Journey I* would soon reach the rendezvous point and complete another critical stage in the test. However, this represented only *half* the test of the space elevator. The last crucial stage—to bring the space pod safely back to earth—still lay ahead. Then, and only then, could LogicTech claim success.

I can't wait to see Gentry's face when that happens!

"How's Bob doing?" Hondo called out. In the muted murmuring within the control room, His friend's voice resounded like a bullhorn. Edison brought up the mannequin's biometrics and peered at the data.

"Bob's simulated vitals are all good...no signs of stress. Atmospheric integrity within the module is also holding steady."

At the sour look on Hondo's face, Edison sighed. "It means Bob is healthy as a horse, and the environmental conditions within the module—oxygen and temperature—are good."

Hondo grinned and flashed a thumbs up.

The sudden blare of a klaxon pierced the muted quiet of the observation tower.

"Reaching geostationary placement," the computer's voice announced. *"Phase one complete."*

"Yes!" Edison cried. All around the control room, LogicTech technicians and employees cheered and high-fived one another. Bree and Carly took turns hugging Edison, while Hondo danced and posed like he just scored a winning touchdown.

The first half of the space elevator test was a success!

Stanton Jones walked over to Edison and placed a hand on his shoulder. With a twinkle in his eye, he said, "Congratulations. Ready to bring *Journey I* home?"

"You bet, Grandpa!"

Edison engaged the program to begin the return sequence.

"Initiating phase two," intoned the simulated voice.

The large screens above the control console displayed the module's progress. As the polarity of the anti-gravity coils reversed, everyone watched *Journey I* make a slow but steady descent back toward earth.

"What's to stop the space pod from dropping like a rock once gravity starts to pull it back to earth?" Bree asked. "I mean, I think I understand how the anti-gravity rings push an object away from earth, but how do you control the return? Then the object is being pulled back to earth by gravity, not pushed."

Edison replied, "Great question, Bree, and actually the most difficult problem to overcome."

Suddenly the center of attention, Bree blushed and stammered, "Uh, it was just something I thought of."

Edison smiled. "The solution was to reverse the polarity of *Journey I's* anti-gravity coils, then a phased reversal of each anti-grav ring in turn. While the rings beneath continue to push against gravity, this produces a gravity brake which slows and decelerates the space pod's descent."

His explanation produced confused looks on his friends' faces. Edison hunted for words to explain what to him was a simple concept. "Okay, imagine a car in drive while you have your foot on the brake," he said. "What happens?"

"The car stops. It doesn't go anywhere," Hondo quipped.

"Exactly. Now, what happens if you ease up on the brake?"

"The car begins to move."

"Yes. Now, picture *Journey I* is the car and each anti-grav disk represents a brake. Once the polarity of *Journey I*'s anti-gravity coils is reversed, she pulls—in conjunction with gravity—back to earth. Visualize further that each ring can also serve as the gas pedal. Once you let off the gas, gravity overcomes the ring's push, and the module begins to fall back to earth. By controlling the energy output of each ring—"

"You're either goosing the gas pedal or letting off on the gas, and the space pod falls faster or slower back to earth," Hondo finished.

"Correct." Edison said, pleased his friend grasped the concept.

"Now you're talking my language! Why can't you explain things like that all the time?"

A piercing alarm rang out before Edison could reply. *Ree, Ree, Ree* it reverberated within the closed confines.

"Gyro malfunction, gyro malfunction," the simulated voice warned.

Galvanized by the siren, Edison's head whipped back to the control console. Technicians rushed to their stations, and the observation tower exploded into frenzied activity.

A technician cried, "A stabilizer gyro on the module has malfunctioned! It's not responding."

"Reboot the program," Edison commanded.

"Already have. It's still not responding."

Edison brought up a virtual schematic of the space pod. The blueprints of *Journey I* hovered before him, and he viewed and discarded each with a flick of his finger.

"Five minutes to total loss of equilibrium!" another technician called out.

Grim-faced, Edison whisked through the schematics with ever increasing speed. Stanton Jones joined Edison to study the blueprints.

Hondo, face pinched in confusion, asked, "Wh-What's going on Mr. Jones?"

"One of the gyros has stopped working. Without it, the module will become unstable and drift out of the space elevator's anti-gravity projection."

Hondo shook his head. "No offense, Mr. Jones, but you sound just like Edison. I don't get what you're saying."

Jones, eyes locked on the continuous stream of schematics flashing by, answered without turning his head. "In order for the anti-gravity rings to work, the polarity or gravity field they produce must be very narrow and tightly focused. Otherwise, the "push" or "pull" is too spread out and too weak to influence an object. Therefore, each anti-gravity ring and *Journey I* have gyros installed to hold and maintain a rigid alignment with each other. If any of the gyros fail, this causes the rings or *Journey I* to move out of alignment, and they fall out of the influence of the space elevator."

"I hate to say I told you so, but this whole test has been an exercise in futility," Gentry commented. He casually strolled toward Jones and smirked at the frenetic activities of Edison and the other LogicTech technicians.

"I'm sorry, Stanton," he continued, "but as you know, there are no shortcuts in science. LogicTech is to be commended for trying—"

"Found it!" Edison cried.

He enlarged the virtual schematic and pointed at a small section pulsing in red. "The chip which controls the energy flow to one of the gyros stopped working. My trouble-shooting program indicates it has inadequate insulation. It's frozen!"

"What? How'd that happen?" Hondo blurted.

"In space, temperatures exist at *absolute zero*," Edison explained as he worked to reestablish control over the gyro. "That means it is at *minus 273 degrees Celsius*. Without adequate insulation, at such low temperatures even molecules stop moving. That means no energy or electricity can reach the gyro to power it."

The atmosphere of the control room went from hopeful to grim resignation.

Stanton Jones shook his head at the bad news. Gentry took Edison's analysis with a smug look of satisfaction.

After a few more moments of furious data-crunching, Edison turned to Stanton Jones. "Grandpa, I think I know how to bring *Journey I* safely back to earth. But it will mean turning off *Journey I*'s program to give me manual control."

Jones frowned. "Why? What would that accomplish?"

"Three of the four gyros are still functioning. If I can increase their power and reconfigure their functions, it's possible to overcome the loss of the other gyro and maintain *Journey I*'s equilibrium."

"*Theoretically* possible, you mean," Jones pointedly corrected Edison. "Why not let the computer recalibrate the power levels to do exactly what you describe?"

"Not enough time, Grandpa. We have less than two minutes to make corrections before the space pod falls out of alignment, and once that happens, it's too late. We can't input and upload data and program changes on the computer before our two minutes are up."

Stanton Jones, arms crossed, tapped his chin and considered Edison's proposal. Finally, he barked, "Parker!"

A technician jumped up from where he was seated on the far end of the control tower. "Yes, sir."

"I understand you're on the Deadman's Switch. When and if I give the signal, you are to engage the self-destruct protocol." With a grim nod, the technician returned to his seat.

Jones turned to Edison. "Okay, Edison. *Journey I* is all yours. But if it looks like you can't keep her aligned with the space elevator rings, I can't let her re-enter the earth's atmosphere and take a chance of striking a populated area.

"I'll have no choice but to blow her up."

CHAPTER 22

Gentry, enjoying the show immensely, didn't notice Carney until the burly bodyguard sidled up next to him and asked, "How about a friendly wager?"

"Pardon? What are you talking about?" Gentry asked, irritated his attention had been diverted from the frantic activities.

"I'm talking about a bet. For example, I'll bet five hundred dollars Edison pulls this off and brings *Journey I* safely back home."

Gentry looked at Carney as if he had just grown a third eye in the middle of his forehead. "You can't be serious."

"Dead serious. And here's the proof." Carney pulled a money clip from his pocket and peeled off five, one hundred dollar bills.

Gentry smirked at the sight of the bills. "If I didn't know better, I'd say the air in here is as thin as in outer space. However, if you're determined to give away your money…"

Gentry pulled out his wallet and matched Carney's five hundred dollars. "Easiest money I've ever made," he quipped.

Both men turned their attention to Edison.

The success or failure of the space elevator was now in his hands.

Edison turned back to his control panel with grim determination.

Four projections now appeared on the big screens. Three displayed the power levels of the remaining gyros, with one displaying the alignment of the anti-grav rings and the module. Much like the "bubble" on a carpenter's level, *Journey 1* already teetered dangerously close to drifting completely off center.

Drops of perspiration beaded Edison's forehead. One particularly bothersome drop began a slow descent down his cheek but Edison couldn't take the time to wipe his face, nor allow himself to divert his attention for one instant from the task at hand.

If *Journey I* tumbled out of control, she would be destroyed. His anti-grav elevator would be a flop, and Gentry would gloat. Everyone would know he failed.

Worse, Carly would know Edison had failed.

The interior of the control tower became quiet as a tomb. In the hushed silence, all eyes watched Edison struggle to keep the space pod from tumbling out of control. Occasionally, *Ree, Ree, Ree* erupted to break the silence when *Journey I* drifted out of alignment. Each time, Edison managed to recalibrate the three remaining gyros and bring the module back.

Although only fifteen minutes elapsed since Edison took over manual control, it felt like hours. Mentally, he struggled to remain focused and keep his responses sharp. Suddenly, a warm hand gently dabbed the beads of sweat from his face with a soft tissue. Startled, Edison spared a quick glance.

Bree stood beside him, a clutch of tissues in her hand.

"You can do it. I know you can, Edison," she whispered.

Bree's faith in him had a galvanizing effect. It flowed through him like an adrenaline rush. *She's right. I can do this.*

Edison re-joined the battle with a ferocity even the fiercest, most competitive linebacker in the NFL would find difficult to match.

"Is he going to be able to pull this off, Mr. Jones?" Hondo asked.

Stanton Jones took his time before answering. "You see that chair over there?" he asked pointing to an empty seat. The friends nodded and he continued, "Now, imagine it has only *three* legs instead of four. What Edison is attempting is like balancing a chair on three legs—possible but difficult. With only three functioning gyros, *Journey* behaves like she has only three legs. Keeping her aligned is an almost impossible task."

"But he's done it so far," Hondo pointed out.

"Yes, he has. However, as *Journey* descends back to earth, the closer she gets, the stronger the pull of gravity. It becomes more difficult, not less."

Silence returned, attention riveted on the monitor showing *Journey I*'s decent. Thick and palpable, the hush broken only by technicians calling out status reports. The sporadic, *Ree, Ree, Ree*, shrieked, triggering frantic efforts by Edison and the LogicTech technicians to bring the space pod back into alignment. Gradually, *Journey I* continued her descent.

An hour passed and the space pod passed through the exosphere and began its descent through the thermosphere. Another half-hour took *Journey I* past the thermosphere.

Then the mesosphere.

Then the stratosphere.

The alarm shrieked so often now, nobody paid attention to it and focused instead, on the monitor tracking the module's descent. When the space pod reached the troposphere, the screeching alarm became continuous and Edison finally shut it off completely.

The final ten kilometer descent through the troposphere was the longest in Edison's life. *Journey I* repeatedly threatened to tilt off balance and fall completely out of the narrow artificial gravity field of the space elevator. Each time, Edison's desperate efforts managed to recalibrate the gyros and steady the module. Each time, the technician fingering the self-destruct button breathed an audible sigh of relief and eased pressure off the switch.

Five kilometers.

Four kilometers.

Three kilometers.

Two kilometers.

One kilometer

Hondo pointed skyward through the tinted windows of the control tower. "Look! I can see her!" he shouted.

High above, barely a pinprick, was *Journey I*. The module wobbled and yawed as it grew larger with each passing second.

Blood pounded inside Edison's temple, and he matched each oscillation with adjustments to the remaining gyros. The delicate balancing act continued until the space pod hovered a meager one hundred yards above the concrete tarmac. Now in a continuous side-to-side fluctuation, the module resembled a spinning top about to topple over and crash to the hard concrete below.

LogicTech security poured out and surrounded the launch pad. Emergency crews and vehicles, already in position, were poised to deal with the potential crash of the space pod.

The module drifted downward closer and closer until it passed at eye level to the control tower.

No one spoke. No one breathed.

Now, mere feet from the tarmac's surface, the descent continued...then it was over. The module settled unsteadily on the hard concrete.

Edison successfully brought *Journey I* home.

Exhausted by the ordeal, Edison laid his head down on the cool metallic surface of the control console. Only vaguely aware of the unrestrained shouts and celebration going on around him, he was convinced no marathon runner or extreme sport athlete could possibly feel as fatigued as he did now. Wearily, he pushed himself up and spotted Carney stride quickly over to Cutter Gentry.

Carney held out his hand. "Time to pay up!"

Gentry, mouth twisted, hesitated before slapping the money in Carney's palm.

"This doesn't change anything, Caruso," the NASA official snapped. "One successful test proves nothing. Countless others will have to be run before NASA gives this so-called 'space elevator' its seal of approval. Oh, and I'll be sure to include in my report this test launch was far from flawless. You can depend on that!"

Carney grinned. "Well, I guess that's part of your job, isn't it? Just be sure to include in your report the twelve-year old boy who pulled the whole thing off from start to finish."

Gentry's facial muscles twitched. He spun on his heel and stalked toward the elevator.

"Oh, and Gentry?" Carney called out.

The NASA official paused and looked back. "What?" he snarled.

"Easiest money I've ever made."

Gentry's face turned purple, the veins on his neck bulging. He managed to turn away, and stalk to the now open elevator. The door closed and the NASA official disappeared from sight.

Carney winked at Edison as he propelled his hoverchair over to his friends and joined the celebration.

The enormity of what had been accomplished began to sink in, and fatigue fell off Edison's shoulders. *Gentry can write whatever he wants in his report. I don't care.*

It wouldn't change the fact for the first time in history, a successful launch of a space elevator took place, and he, Edison Jones, had been part of it!

CHAPTER 23

HONDO STARED AT THE PIECE OF PAPER IN HIS HANDS.

His mid-term progress report showed passing grades in all his classes save one. The "50" in science jumped off the page like a bullseye. His shoulders slumped. The "50" average made it impossible to pass for the six week term. Not this time. With less than three weeks left, even if he made A's and B's on every assignment, he would fall far short of the "70" required to pass.

He would lose his academic eligibility—which meant no more football.

There were four weeks left in the football season with a bye this week. That meant three games left, including the season finale against the Paris Wildcats. Paris, district football champions five years in a row, were unbeaten. No one could remember the last time Harpersville defeated the Wildcats—at any level. If Harpersville and Paris won their next two games, the two undefeated teams would play for the district championship.

And I'll be benched for the most important game of the season!

The bell rang, rescuing Hondo from his gloomy thoughts. The progress report clutched in his fist, he made his way out of class and into the hallway. Hondo stopped, lost in thought about his predicament. Like a boulder in a swift moving stream, students flowed around his large body as they hurried on their way. Jaw clenched,

Hondo turned and quickly made his way toward his science class.

Shouldering his way past students, Hondo approached his teacher. "Mr. Russell, can I talk to you for a second?"

Mr. Russell looked up from his desk, the progress report held before him in Hondo's hand. With a nod, he said, "Sure, Hondo. But I don't think you will like what I have to say."

"Isn't there anything I can do to bring up my science grade?" Hondo pleaded. "I have to be eligible for the last game against Paris."

Mr. Russell sighed and turned his attention to his computer. A few clicks of the keyboard later, Hondo's grades appeared. He studied them for a few moments then shook his head.

"Yes, there were some things you could have done to bring your grade up. For example, you could actually *study* for a test. Or you could retake the tests you failed to try and improve your grade…except you never show up. Last—and here's a truly novel idea—you could turn in your assignments instead of taking a zero on them."

Hondo brightened. "Hey, I can do that. No problem! I'll get right on it!"

"Actually, there is a big problem. You see, these are all things you should have done *before* you received your progress report. You don't have enough time now." Mr. Russell leaned back in his chair. "And I'm not going to reward your lack of effort now that you are finally concerned about your grades."

Mr. Russell tapped his pen on the top of his desk. "I'm sorry, Hondo, I just don't see how you can pass this six weeks. You can't make up in two weeks what you refused to do the previous four weeks."

"That's not fair!" Hondo cried. "I said I'd make up all the work!"

Mr. Russell frowned and gave the pen one final tap.

"Look, I know how much football means to you. I know the seventh-grade team has a chance to be the district champions for the first time in years…it's all over the school and it's all anybody can talk about. But I can't let you or any other student cut corners because you are inconvenienced or might lose your eligibility. That's not how education works, and that's not how *life* works."

"Just give me a chance—"

Mr. Russell held up his hand. "No, Hondo. I'm not changing my mind. But, what I will do is give you every opportunity to pass in the time you have left in this grade term." He crossed his arms. "I'm sorry. It's the best I can do."

Hondo, jaw clenched, stood silently for a moment, then spun on his heel and stalked out of the room. At the door, a display on the bulletin board caught his eye. He'd walked by the same display dozens of times and it never registered with him. Now, however, as he studied it, a wide grin grew on his face. The title of the display read:

Regional Robotics Competition

Hondo snatched a brochure from the small table beneath the bulletin board, and scanned it quickly. His thoughts transformed from grim to joyful.

"Yes!" he cried.

Hondo ran back to Mr. Russell's desk. He put the brochure down, flattened it out, then pointed to a section at the bottom of the flyer.

"It says here anyone entering the robotics competition receives a project grade…which counts as a test grade. If I entered the competition, I'd get a test grade, right?"

Mr. Russell lifted an eyebrow and cocked his head. "Yes, but the deadline is two days from now. That's only two days to provide an entry."

Ticking off points on his fingers, the science teacher continued, "You would have to find at least four other students because the minimum team is five. Then you would have to order the robotics kit which costs money...a minimum of $2,500. Although we received a grant to help pay for some of the program, students are supposed to secure business sponsorships to pay for the kit. Once the kit is received, the robot has to be built, tested, programmed, and presented for competition."

Finally," Mr. Russell said holding up a last finger, "the regional competition is three weeks from now. Most of the robotic teams from other schools have been working on their robots since the summer. You couldn't possibly pull this off in three weeks. You don't have enough time."

"But if I *can* get it done in time do I get the grade?" Hondo persisted.

Mr. Russell threw up his hands. "Okay, yes, Hondo. *If* you enter a project in time, *if* you can pay for and receive a kit, and *if* you can construct a robot in time for the competition, then you would earn the grade."

Hondo whooped. "Thanks, Mr. Russell. That's all I wanted to hear!"

Hondo ran out into the hallway and celebrated like he just scored a winning touchdown. The look on Mr. Russell's face when he asked about the robotics competition caused him to laugh out loud. He must have thought Hondo popped a screw loose.

But he had a secret weapon.

He had Edison Jones!

"Are you kidding me, Hondo?"

Edison rubbed his eyes and stared at his friend. "The contest is in *three* weeks!" The two sat at a table in the cafeteria as students milled around them carrying lunch trays. Edison held the robotics pamphlet in one hand and continued to study it carefully.

"So? I need the contest to be in three weeks, otherwise I won't be eligible for the football game against Paris."

"Look, the kit hasn't even been ordered. That'll take days. And the robotics team is supposed to have five members. Where will you get the other four members on such short notice?"

Hondo scratched his chin. "Well, besides you and me, I thought maybe Bree and Carly. That's four. I'm still working on the fifth person, but I'll think of somebody."

Edison sighed, and dropped the brochure onto the table. "This is going to be difficult. There's very little time left, and I don't know if we can pull it off. If we just had more time…" Hondo's stony expression answered this pronouncement.

Edison swallowed, then pointed at a particular section on the flyer. "The kit costs over two thousand dollars and not only should it have been ordered months ago, but we're supposed to have secured business donations to pay for it."

Hondo's face reddened. "Okay, okay! You sound like Mr. Russell. 'It's impossible,' 'not enough time,' 'not enough money.' Look, I'll see you around!"

Edison caught Hondo's arm as he spun and started to stalk off.

"I didn't say impossible. I said it would be difficult. As far as the money for the kit…well, some of the computer components on *Journey I* cost ten times as much. I think you know money isn't going to be an issue."

Edison felt the tension ease from his friend's arm. Hondo looked over at him. "I'll pay you back. When I'm older and can get a job, I'll pay—"

Edison waved his hand. "Don't worry about."

Edison moved his anti-grav chair to face Hondo. "You're my friend. The money—it's not important. Having you as a friend is important. So, of course, I'll help you."

"Thanks. Sorry for getting mad," Hondo mumbled.

Edison chuckled. "No problem, but if we're going to do this, I do have one requirement."

Hondo blinked. "What is it?"

"*You* are going to help me every step of the way. Assembling the robot, programming it, testing it. This is your project, Hondo, and I hope it teaches you something."

"You mean about building robots?"

"No, I mean not getting into a mess like this again. Study and turn in your homework!"

Hondo grinned. "Bro, that's cold-blooded. Can't make any promises, but don't worry. I'll pull my weight on this project."

Edison shook his head and eyed Hondo. "Well, I guess we need to get started then. You find Carly and Bree and recruit them for the team. I'm going to find Mr. Russell and ask him a few more questions before I order the robotics kit. Soon as football practice is over, Carney will pick you up so be ready."

Hondo moaned. "Already?"

With a snort, Edison pivoted his hoverchair and propelled it toward the cafeteria exit. Hondo hurried after Edison.

"Ah, so you're not kidding? We're starting today?"

Mario sat alone and watched them leave. Despite the crowded cafeteria, no one chose to sit anywhere near him. Unbeknownst to Edison and Hondo, he had listened to and followed their conversation closely.

He got up and dumped his tray. Moments after he vacated the table, it immediately filled up with students. Mario went in search of Markie Franks.

Maybe I can get a second chance after all.

CHAPTER 24

Mario found Markie smoking a cigarette and lounging with the other members of his gang in the same spot where Edison had blown his clothes off with the vortex cannon. Markie tracked his progress through narrowed eyes. With a deft flick of his wrist, he sent the cigarette butt flying through the air.

It rolled to a stop at Mario's feet.

He gave Mario a menacing look. "Watcha doing here? Ya need another ass whupping?"

Mario gulped, the gang forming a circle around him. His tongue seemed to stick to his mouth when he tried to form the words to tell Markie what he had overheard.

"Hey, uh, I heard Jones and Edwards talking about something. It sounded kinda important, and um, I thought you might, uh, want to know about it," he chattered.

"That so?" Markie moved closer until he towered directly over the smaller boy. He leaned to within inches of Mario's face. "Now what exactly would that be?"

The stale odor of cigarettes on his breath soured Mario's stomach. His mouth opened and shut convulsively, but try as he might, no sound would come out of his constricted throat.

Impatient, Markie put a large hand on Mario's shoulder. He squeezed until a yelp of pain exploded from the smaller boy's mouth. "Talk!" he barked.

Like a breached dam, the words broke from Mario's lips. "Jones and Edwards…they-they're forming a robot team or something!"

"And why should I care?" Markie snarled. He savagely squeezed Mario's shoulder again.

Crying out, tears rolled down Mario's cheeks.

"Be-because Edwards needs the robot team to pass!" Mario sobbed. "It's a project and he needs the grade to keep from failing science. If he doesn't pass, then he can't play football."

Markie stiffened at this information. A cunning smile appeared on his lips.

He released Mario, then leaned to eye level with him.

"Start from the beginning…and tell me *everything*."

"What's that?"

Hondo pointed at a crate on Edison's large workbench. They were in the underground lab where they had gone immediately after football practice.

A plate stacked high with ham and cheese sandwiches also lay on the bench. Both boys helped themselves. Edison swallowed a bite and said, "It's the robotics kit, along with some other components I thought we might need."

Hondo almost choked. "What? How did you get it so quickly? You said it would take days."

Edison shrugged. "A LogicTech employee picked it up from the manufacturer and I had it flown directly here. It arrived an hour or so ago."

Hondo shook his head. "You weren't kidding when you said we were going to get started right away."

Edison took another bite from his sandwich. Chewing, he nodded. "Just like I wasn't kidding when I said *you* are going to work on this every step of the way. Did you talk to Carly and Bree about being on the team?"

Hondo sighed. *Can't we have at least one free day before we have to start on the robot project?*

He picked up a sandwich in one large hand, and it disappeared in two bites. Around a mouthful of ham and cheese, he said, "Yep. Carly jumped at the chance. After Bree gave me a speech about responsibility, yada, yada, she said she would be on the team also. Now all we need is one more."

"Good. The first thing you can do is unpack that crate and spread everything out so we can do an inventory. Then text Carly and Bree and ask them if they can start tomorrow."

Hondo brushed the bread crumbs off his T-shirt and pulled out his cell phone. He quickly fired off a text to both girls. He picked up a box cutter, and with a sigh, eyed the plastic-wrapped crate.

Time to get to work.

"This is all so exciting!" Carly bubbled.

All four friends were gathered around Edison's work bench. Neatly arranged before them were all the parts from the robotics kit. A virtual image of the components hovered above them, each labeled for easy identification and reference.

Bree studied the virtual display floating before them. "I like how you have each part labeled. It will make it easier when we start to assemble the robot."

Hondo snorted. "Easier? Are you kidding? I had to unload

and arrange every part from the kit. Then Edison made me input the data to label each part into the computer. I bet it was midnight before we finished!"

Hondo yawned and stretched. "I'm thinking, good thing it's Friday. Since I'm spending the night, we can sleep in on Saturday. So what happens? Edison is shaking me awake at the crack of dawn so we can get back to work!"

Carly sidled next to Hondo. A Styrofoam cup of Chai tea perched in one hand, she looped her other hand around Hondo's arm.

"Whatever I—I mean *we*—need to do to help you pass science, all you have to do is ask. Right, Bree?" Carly looked over her shoulder at Bree.

Bree rolled her eyes. "Oh, yes. *Definitely!*"

The sight of Carly snuggled next to Hondo triggered a return of Edison's irrational jealousy. Like a monster from the deep, it arose to temporarily distract him. The fact Hondo seemed oblivious to the attention only served to make this jealousy sharper and more pointed.

Edison gritted his teeth and managed to force himself to concentrate on the task at hand. "Let's get started."

He maneuvered the anti-grav chair alongside the workbench, then turned to face his friends.

"The robot consists of a brain or C-RIO, a motor on wheels called a jagwire which regulates voltage to the robot's transmission, a 12-volt battery to supply power, and a frame made of aluminum." Edison caused each of the assembled components to glow brightly on the virtual display.

"Now, each school's robotics team receives the same basic robotics kit. Each team can spend up to an additional $2,500 to soup up their robot, but the rules say no robot can weigh more than 150 pounds."

Edison grinned. "Obviously, I have a few ideas on how to improve our robot."

"So, that's it? You just build a better robot?" Hondo asked.

"Nope. That's only part of it…the *easy* part."

Hondo groaned. "I knew it. More work!"

Edison ignored his friend and continued. "The actual competition is divided into two parts. The first part consists of the robot working autonomously at a task. The second part of the competition requires an operator to direct and control the robot at a task. Of course, I'll program the robot for the autonomous operation."

Edison turned and pointed at Hondo. "But *you* will be the robot operator."

Hondo gulped. "Me?"

"You," Edison repeated firmly.

The stricken expression on Hondo's face caused Edison to laugh. Soon Bree joined in and even Carly began to giggle.

Hondo scratched his head. "So, what's this task the robot's supposed to do?"

"Good question," Edison replied, enjoying his friend's discomfort.

"This year's task is to put balls through a hoop, much like a basketball. Each robot has one minute and forty-five seconds to put as many balls through the goal as possible. That's the fifteen second autonomous operation, and the ninety seconds of operator control.

Since this information was released to schools back in January, most teams have been working on their robots ever since—and the robotics competition is only three weeks from today at the Dallas Convention Center."

Edison looked at his friends. "This means they have an eight month head start on us. We have less than three weeks to prepare our own robot. We'll have to work night and day to even have a chance."

Edison folded his arms. "Everybody good with that?"

Hondo looked like he swallowed a football but managed a nod. Bree and Carly soon followed as well.

Edison rubbed his hands eagerly.

"Right...let's get to work!"

CHAPTER 25

Edison had barely exited his math class when he heard his name called out.

"C'mon!" Hondo yelled.

Edison blinked. Even with milling students in the densely packed hallway, he spotted Hondo towering over everybody else. His friend motioned frantically.

Edison frowned. "What?" He called out.

Pushing his way through clusters of students, Hondo stood beside Edison. A palpable look of excitement covered his face.

"We gotta go to Mr. Russell's room *now*! He's got someone who wants to be on the robotics team!"

That's why he is so worked up.

"Okay. Let's go."

Today marked the last day to submit the names of Harpersville's robotics team. No one wanted to commit to what would be three weeks of intense work to prepare for the competition. No amount of begging and arm-twisting by Carly, Bree, and Hondo had succeeded in persuading another student to join them.

Five team members were needed by the end of the day, or it would all be over.

Edison hesitated. "Let me tell my Texas History teacher I might be late to class."

Hondo gestured. *"C'mon.* Mr. Russell will give you a hall pass. Your streak of *never* being late is safe!"

Edison sighed. He turned the hoverchair to follow Hondo who had already rounded the corner. Maneuvering his anti-grav chair through the heavy student traffic, he finally reached the science lab. He glided through the doorway to where Hondo stood next to Mr. Russell.

"We're here, Mr. Russell!" Hondo exclaimed. "Who have you got for the robotics team?"

Mr. Russell chuckled. "Well, I see you didn't waste any time after you got my message."

The science teacher pointed to the back of the classroom where a stocky boy stood. Back turned to them, he studied the skeleton of a frog mounted on a pedestal inside a glass case. The boy struck Edison as familiar, and when he turned around, his heart sank.

Markie Franks!

Edison's stomach clenched like a vise, and he felt nauseous. His reaction, however, paled in comparison to Hondo's.

At first, his friend wore an expression of incomprehension then disbelief, and finally, anger. "Franks!" The name ripped from Hondo's lips.

"Nice to see you too, Edwards," Markie sneered.

Oblivious to the thick animosity, Mr. Russell said, "Oh, good. It seems you know each other."

"Yeah, we know it each other all right. Enough to know he can't be on our team!"

Mr. Russell rubbed his chin while he looked from one boy to the other. His eyes widened. "Oh."

The science teacher coughed. "Um, er, I see. Well, Hondo, the problem we have is the rules clearly state you must have a minimum of five team members. Today is the deadline, and without five students, you simply can't enter the competition."

Mr. Russell raised an eyebrow. "Do you have another student who wants to be part of your group?"

Hondo dropped his eyes and shook his head.

"Then I don't see how you have a—"

"I don't care! Franks isn't going to be on the team!"

Markie shrugged. "That's okay, Mr. Russell. I thought if I could get in on this robot thing, it would help my grade. But if Edwards doesn't want me…" He grabbed his backpack and started to the door.

"Markie, stop!" Edison cried. He moved his hoverchair to block the door. "We'll take Markie, Mr. Russell."

"Edison, no!" Hondo cried. "He'll mess things up on purpose!"

"We don't have a choice." Edison turned. "Besides, everybody deserves a second chance, right Markie?"

A cunning smile appeared on Markie's face. "Oh, yeah. I'm *all* about second chances, Jones."

A strained silence followed, broken when Mr. Russell cleared his throat.

"Right. I'll add Markie's name and your team will be set." Mr. Russell pointed at Hondo. "Any questions?"

Jaw clenched, Hondo gave a curt shake of his head.

"Good." The science teacher grabbed a pad from his desk and quickly scribbled tardy passes for the three boys.

The deserted corridors, calm now, echoed with the boys' footsteps and the hum of Edison's anti-grav chair. Once they turned the corner and were out of sight of the science lab, Hondo whirled on Markie.

"Screw this up, and I'll *personally* make sure you regret it!" he hissed.

"Shut up, Edwards!" Markie snarled. "You don't scare me! You can take your so-called warning and shove it up—"

"Stop it!" Edison cried.

Edison looked around, relieved no one heard them. He whispered, "Look, Hondo, we *need* Markie. We can't field a team without him. Let's just try to do the best we can."

Markie smiled, teeth exposed like a shark preparing to bite. "Yeah, Edwards. You need me. Otherwise, no project grade and you fail science. Wouldn't it be a damn shame if you couldn't play the last football game of the season? And with everybody counting on you? I know I would be *very* disappointed."

Hondo, red-faced, stepped toward Markie. Edison quickly zipped his hoverchair between them.

"Calm down, Hondo. Just calm down," Edison pleaded.

Markie studied his nails. "The way I see it, if I ever choose to quit, you and your robotics team are sunk, plain and simple."

He dropped his hand. Eyes narrowed, he said, "So here's how things will go down. I'll play along, but only the way I want to do it! Don't hassle me, don't bug me, and most of all, don't expect me to do much."

Markie glared at Hondo. "I'll get a grade which will help me pass science, and now that you have your precious robotics team, you get to keep playing the big, football hero."

Markie barked a laugh. "Oh, and just for the record? I don't give a rat's ass about whether this robotics team does well or not, and I certainly don't care whether Edwards ever plays another football game."

He jerked his chin at Hondo. "What I do care about is that you stop ragging me and keep your mouth shut!"

Markie pointed at Edison. "So you better make sure your friend keeps his maggot mouth under control, otherwise I walk. Understand?"

Markie spun on his heel and stalked off.

"It's not worth it!" Hondo managed to spit through gritted

teeth. "Markie deserves an ass-kicking, and I'm going to give it to him!"

For a second time, Edison grabbed Hondo to restrain him.

"*Think!*" he hissed. "Would you calm down long enough to think about your situation?" Edison could feel his friend's muscles tense through his shirt, but he made no move to go after Markie.

Relieved, Edison quickly added, "Look, you got me into this so you could pass science and be eligible for football. Have you changed your mind?"

Hondo shook his head.

"Then we need Markie! Don't you see we have no choice? There *is* no one else. Who cares if he doesn't help or do any of the work? He makes number five and that's *all* that counts!"

Hondo's shoulders slumped. "I guess you're right. But you know he'll try to screw things up, sabotage the robot or something."

Edison shrugged. "It's just one more variable to deal with. And since we know what he's like, we can plan for it."

A grunt escaped from Hondo. "Never heard Franks described as a 'variable' before. That's funny. I'd call him an—"

"Never mind!" Edison hastily interjected. "The important thing is we have our team and we can get started."

"Yeah. I guess so. Look, I gotta get to class. See ya'." Hondo trudged off.

After his friend disappeared around a corner, Edison directed his anti-grav chair down the empty hallway.

A persistent itch scratched between his shoulder blades as he made his way to his own class—like an ill premonition of things to come. Although Edison put no stock in such things, he couldn't shake the feeling.

It remained with him the rest of the day.

CHAPTER 26

Not much was accomplished the first day the whole robotics team—including Markie—met in Edison's lab.

When Carney picked them all up after school in a LogicTech company van, the problems started immediately.

Markie pushed past Hondo to sit next to Carly, which led Hondo to flank her other side. Carly ended up wedged between them like a slice of cheese. This forced Bree to sit alone in one of the big back seats while Edison perched in the front seat next to Carney.

Markie and Hondo took turns glaring at each other, broken only intermittently when Markie chose to leer at Carly. The tense atmosphere made the normally fifteen minute drive feel like hours. When they finally arrived at the Jones Mansion, Edison, in his haste to exit the van, had to restrain himself from lunging into his anti-grav chair and speeding away.

Markie stepped out, stretched, and made a show of studying the house and grounds. "You got quite a spread here, Jones. Must be nice to be rich."

Carney stood nearby, and Edison shrugged at his *I hope you know what you're doing* look, and seriously began to doubt the wisdom of including Markie on the team—even if it meant Hondo failed science and couldn't play football.

He gulped and glided past the doors.

As they filed through, Markie quipped, "What, no butler?"

Once inside, he stopped and stood hands on hips. He blinked at the sight of the staircase and balustrade, then stared at the enormous chandelier hanging from the ceiling.

He whistled. "Just how rich are you, Jones? I bet the toilets here are all gold-plated." Markie snickered at his little joke, then sauntered up to one of the large paintings on the wall and pretended to study it.

"Yes, I do believe these brush strokes are inconsistent with the media being used. How droll. How positively droll!"

Hondo sidled up next to Edison. "He's pissing me off! I don't even know what 'droll' means, but it still pisses me off!"

"Let's just get this over with," Edison managed to say. He propelled his hoverchair up the stairs and led the team to the elevator.

Edison derived some satisfaction at the look of fear on Markie's face when the pneumatic car dropped to take them down the twenty stories to his lab.

Hondo wore a broad grin. "What's the matter, Franks? You look a little shook up."

The elevator hissed to a stop. Carly and Bree stifled a giggle when Markie, his face pale, stumbled from his seat and rushed out the open doors.

Markie, breathing heavily, quickly recovered. "No problem, Edwards. No problem at all." He walked further into Edison's lab and scanned the cavernous chamber.

"Impressive, Jones," he grunted. He followed the others to a large workbench where the robot's components were carefully laid out.

Edison stopped and wheeled to face the team. "Okay, we have three weeks to get our robot assembled and programmed. Is everybody ready?" His friends nodded. Markie snorted.

Ignoring him, Edison said, "Okay. Let's get started."

Edison assigned each person to a task, and the rest of the evening passed uneventfully. Bree and Hondo assembled the robot's frame, with Carly and Markie handing them the proper tools and components. Edison kept one eye on them as he worked on the robot's programming. Frequent stops were common. Either Bree and Hondo were stumped on how to assemble components like the wiring harness, or Carly and Markie couldn't find a correct part or tool. Edison would then have to help them until they could successfully complete the task.

Their progress went in ebbs and flows.

For the most part Markie behaved himself, although he chose to stand so close to Carly, she finally put a chair between them. A short time later Markie "accidentally" broke one of the eight wheels being attached to the robot's frame.

He shrugged. "Oops." Fortunately, they had extra wheels, so it didn't slow their progress.

Eventually, Markie became bored with the slow proceedings. He took a hard rubber ball from his pocket and threw it against the concrete wall of the lab. The impact echoed in the air, and he amused himself by continuing to throw and catch while the others worked.

No one tried to get Markie to rejoin them.

They called it a night after nine and took the pneumatic elevator back up to the mansion. Carney waited for them in the van, and the trip back to town was made without incident. The mental toll in assembling the robot exhausted them. Even Markie spent his time quietly staring at the darkened countryside through the van's windows.

Carney dropped off each member of the robotics team at their home. Edison had never seen Bree's house, an attractive two story brick home with a huge oak tree in the middle of the front lawn. Markie's house surprised Edison. Although more modest than Bree's, it was also a brick home with an immaculate yard and appearance. He wasn't sure what he expected—maybe a mobile home with rusting cars on blocks in the yard—not the tidy home the bully lived in.

Hondo, the last person they dropped off, *did* live in a mobile home complete with a yard full of foot-high weeds. The only light came from the blue flicker of a TV through a grimy window next to the front door. With a grimace, Hondo got out and waved, his shoes pushing a path through the brown weeds and grass.

Edison, thankful Carney chose not to quiz him about Markie, hoped in the days ahead they could make better headway. Tomorrow would come soon enough, and the team would be hard at it again. And on a Saturday no less!

He stifled a groan at the thought of an even longer day with Markie. His presence filled the air with such tension, it lay on all of them like a heavy blanket. *Maybe Hondo is right. Maybe it's not worth it.*

The scene of a teary-eyed, humiliated Markie in only his boxer shorts, suddenly played through Edison's mind. Guilt weighed heavily on him, and Edison finally managed to banish the unwelcome vision. Markie would remain a part of the team he decided.

For my sake as well as Hondo's.

CHAPTER 27

To the immense relief of Edison and the rest of the robotics team, Markie didn't show up Saturday morning to resume the work on their project.

An almost festive atmosphere took over the operation, and Team Edison managed to get much more accomplished than the evening before. Markie was also a no-show after school on Monday, and only "helped" with the project two days the entire week.

No one complained.

The days flew by, and progress on the robot continued until the only thing left was to field test the robot and tweak the programming.

During this time, the seventh-grade football team won both of its games with ease, 38-7 against the Pine Tree Pirates, and 32-14 against the Sulphur Springs Wildcats. Hondo dazzled at quarterback and anchored a stifling defense from his linebacker position. Paris also won both of its games to set up an epic district championship game at Harpersville the week after the regional robotics competition.

Now all Hondo had to do was pass science.

"Okay, is everybody ready?" Edison called out.

Hondo rubbed his neck and flashed a thumbs up, while Bree and Carly fidgeted beside him.

Markie—a no-show again for the final day of tests and trial runs—meant Team Edison could breathe a sigh of relief. Physically and mentally wrung out from the non-stop work on their project, the hulking bully's absence lowered everyone's stress level. With only three weeks to play catch up, it took every bit of Edison's technological genius to allow them to accomplish what normally took other teams months.

The moment of truth had arrived and Edison was eager to test their robot. "Okay team, today is Thursday, and tomorrow we leave for Dallas. Regionals take place Saturday at the Convention Center. Any questions?"

"Nope. You, er, I mean, we got this," Hondo answered.

Edison propelled his hoverchair forward to stop next to Hondo. He handed him a black, portable, remote unit.

"Good. That means you're up."

Hondo gulped.

His hands shook as he took the remote. "Hope I don't mess up."

Edison flashed his big friend a smile. "You'll do just fine. As the robot controller, all you'll need to do is follow the sequence we've practiced dozens of times."

"Yeah, but you always helped me," Hondo grumbled.

He fingered the remote. "Now I'm going to have to do it all by myself."

Hondo took a deep breath and gripped the controller with sweat-slicked hands.

My first time to direct the robot all by myself.

Under Edison's watchful eye, Hondo had practiced over and over again to refine his technique until the robot responded flawlessly to his commands.

I can do this, he told himself. *I don't need Edison anymore.* Still, his heart thumped while he went through the pre-drill routine Edison pounded into him.

Power on. *Check!*

Signal strength—excellent. *Check!*

Programming—enabled. *Check!*

Battery—fully charged. *Check!*

Servo-motors—all in the green. *Check!*

Football is easy compared to this, Hondo decided. He wiped his hands on his pants. Manipulating the remote, he started the robot and it trundled toward a corner of Edison's lab.

There, they had constructed a replica of the "pit" all the robots in the competition were required to perform in. It resembled a cage surrounding a pair of basketball goals. The fencing was twelve feet high and covered with a type of nylon netting similar to that on batting cages. One section was left open in order to let the robot enter.

Of the two portable basketball goals inside the pit, one stood at nine feet tall, and the other at six feet. Basketball-sized rubber balls filled a bin inside. Hondo had ninety seconds to place as many balls through the hoop as possible.

Hondo released a pent-up breath, then he directed his team's automaton into the cage.

The rules stipulated a weight limit of one hundred and fifty pounds for each robot. This included the twelve-volt battery to power the machine. Its frame and chassis—made of a lightweight aluminum alloy—had been modified to fit four wheels on each side. Capable of a 360 degree range of motion, the wheels allowed the robot to start or stop on a dime, and turn in any direction. The articulated arms had a hinged joint and scalloped, spade-like hands. This design made it easier to scoop up the balls and shoot them—less time wasted meant more shot attempts.

Hondo stopped the robot by the ball bin. He manipulated the automaton's position until it faced the basketball goals. He nodded at Edison.

Edison pointed at a digital clock mounted above the cage. "On my mark, the ninety seconds starts. Keep in mind the taller goal is worth four points per made shot, and the lower goal two points."

Hondo wiped his hands again on his pants and grasped the remote controller firmly.

"Ready, set, *go!*"

The robot pivoted into motion. Metal arms reached into the ball bin and each hand lifted up a ball. Hondo directed the robot to shoot one, then another at the nine foot goal.

Both missed badly.

Grimacing, Hondo made a quick adjustment and two more balls rolled into the robot's hands. Each ball in turn flew toward the basketball goal.

More misses, although closer this time.

Hondo stomped his foot and eyed the countdown clock. He made more corrections. Scooping up two more balls, he sent them flying toward the nine-foot goal. Each rubber sphere rolled around the goal—then rimmed out.

Gritting his teeth, Hondo continued to tweak the robot's trajectory with each shot getting closer to the net. He managed two last attempts in the final seconds.

Swish, Swish. Both shots went in.

A loud chime went off. *Time up.*

"Yes! That's what I'm talking about!" Hondo cried. Controller held high in the air, he pumped his fist. Carly and Bree clapped and cheered.

"Let's do it again!"

Edison grinned. "See, I told you. You just needed some live practice. Okay, here we go."

Edison reset the clock. Hondo eyed the digital countdown with raptor-like intensity. When Edison said *go*, he already had the robot reaching for balls. When time ran out, almost half the shots had gone in.

"Again!" Hondo shouted.

With steely determination, Hondo directed the robot like an orchestra conductor, his confidence and expertise growing with each time trial. When the chime sounded this time, over half the rubber balls swished through the hoop.

"Again!"

At the end of the tenth time trial, Hondo jumped up and down, then whooped and danced around Edison's hoverchair.

No misses. *A perfect score!*

Edison high-fived Hondo. "Congratulations!"

A happy grin split Hondo's face. "I had a good teacher. Hey, I'm gonna try shooting at the six-foot goal now."

Hondo scrambled to retrieve the dozens of rubber balls scattered within the cage. Carly joined him, chattering nonstop.

Bree stood beside Edison. "Poor Carly. She talks about Hondo all the time and he barely knows she exists."

She turned to face Edison. "The more Hondo ignores her, the more Carly likes him. I guess that's the weird thing about girls. We like the guys who ignore us. Isn't that funny?"

Edison stared at Bree. His face grew warm as he tried to decipher her comment. He managed to stutter, "Er...I guess."

"You like Carly, don't you?"

Edison froze. "What? No! I mean, yes, everybody likes Carly!" he stammered.

"You know what I mean. You like Carly. I've seen the way you look at her."

Edison's pulse raced, his heart in his throat. He tried several times to formulate a reply...with no success.

Bree crossed her arms. "Do you like me, Edison? Because I know what it's like to be ignored too."

Edison felt like a trapped animal. His first impulse was to flee, to escape. If he had use of his legs, he didn't know if he could have stopped himself from running out of the lab.

"Of course I like you, Bree. You know that," he managed to say. A horrible thought crossed his mind, and a cold shiver traveled down his spine.

"Wait! What are you going to tell Carly? You aren't going to—"

"Your secret is safe with me," Bree said, a finger to her lips.

Bree stepped back. "Well, it looks like Hondo's finished putting all the balls back in the container," she observed—as if their recent conversation had been nothing more than a casual talk about the weather. "Are you ready to reset the timer?"

Numb, Edison nodded. As the digital clock ran down, one overriding thought gripped him.

What just happened?

CHAPTER 28

THE NEXT TWENTY-FOUR HOURS ROCKETED BY IN A BLUR.

Grateful for the quick passage of time, Edison was too busy to think about Bree's comment about liking Carly—or her for that matter! Unlike his grasp of technology, he had sailed into uncharted waters, and *way* out of his element, when it came to girls and their feelings.

There were a million last minute details to deal with. Edison spent much of it on final diagnostic tests of the robot and getting it ready for shipment. Team Edison was booked at a hotel near the Dallas Convention Center, along with Edison's Grandpa and Carney. Carly and Bree's parents planned to drive up the next day to watch the competition.

Hondo never said a word whether his mother planned to attend.

When Mr. Russell pulled the school van out of the Harpersville parking lot and onto the road, Edison breathed a sigh of relief. What started out three weeks ago as a desperate sprint to complete a robotics project—and help Hondo pass science—now had a finish line in sight. A lot could have gone wrong, especially with Markie Franks on the team. Edison still couldn't believe he and Hondo hadn't exchanged punches during the process.

But, despite all the obstacles, they did it!

They assembled a robot, programmed it, tested it, and now had a chance to win the competition.

The trip to Dallas went without incident. Mr. Russell chose to have Markie room with him, and to ride shotgun next to him in the van. Carly's constant chatter and the normal back and forth banter with Hondo and Bree kept the atmosphere within the van tension-free. In fact, the only thing Edison found worrisome was Markie's silence. He said nothing the entire trip, and wore a smug expression—as if he knew a secret the others didn't. Edison decided he was being too hypersensitive, and pushed it out of his mind.

Once Team Edison checked into the hotel and unloaded their luggage, they used their free time to wander about the grounds. Other robotic teams were at the same hotel, and they got a chance to meet and talk with many of them. Carly, in her element, chatted and laughed, a large contingent of boys always surrounding her.

Edison was peppered constantly with questions about his hovering chair. Only a few short months ago, he would have been embarrassed by the attention, particularly his condition of being in a wheelchair. Now he just shrugged it off.

Hondo stood out like a supertanker amongst a sea of rowboats. He plowed through a group of kids to stand beside Edison.

"Help! I'm drowning in geeks. If I get asked another question about which Marvel superhero is my favorite, I'm gonna go nuts! I gotta get out of here."

Edison laughed and they left the crowded lobby.

A hospitality room had been set up within one of the conference rooms, and Hondo, hungry as usual, steered Edison toward it. Tables lined the wall and were loaded with sandwiches, various snack foods, and soft drinks. Hondo wasted little time helping himself. Edison wasn't hungry, so he maneuvered his anti-grav chair off to the side and out of the way. Lost in his thoughts, an unfamiliar voice broke his concentration.

"It's obvious you use some sort of electromagnet to produce an antigravity field, but we're curious about what energy source you use to charge it."

"Yes, we are *very* curious," a second voice chimed in.

"Did you use the same antigravity field when you successfully tested your space elevator?" Two voices asked in unison.

Startled by the rapid-fire questions, Edison looked up. A boy and a girl about his age appeared beside his hoverchair. Both had blonde hair so light in color, it almost appeared white. Fine as straw, it fell to the girl's shoulders, while the boy's reached past his ears to the base of his neck. The twins possessed pallid complexions as if they never got out into the sun, and both wore similar clothing—the girl a black skirt with a white blouse and black shoes, and the boy black trousers, white shirt, black tie, and black shoes. A black blazer with a red and green insignia sewn above the breast pocket completed their ensemble.

They stood at identical height, two pairs of intense blue eyes peered at Edison.

"I see we have surprised you," the girl said when he didn't immediately reply. "A formal introduction is in order. I am Hillary Breakstone."

"And I am Heller Breakstone," the boy added.

"And as you have no doubt surmised," Hillary continued.

"We are twins," Hillary and Heller said in unison.

Edison realized he was gawking. He gulped and managed to say, "Er, pleased to meet you. My name is—"

"Edison Jones," Hillary and Heller finished.

"Yes, how did—"

"Your grandfather, Stanton Jones, is chairman and CEO of LogicTech," Hillary began.

"The largest privately owned technology company in the world," Heller finished.

Dumbfounded, Edison stared at the twins and fumbled for a reply. Hillary continued, "Your parents were killed in a car accident when you were five."

"The same accident fractured your spinal cord," Heller added.

"Thus leaving you a paraplegic from the waist down," the twins chimed.

Speechless, Edison was unaware that Hondo stood beside him, a thick sandwich in one hand and a soft drink in the other, listening to the entire conversation.

A sour look covered his friend's face while he munched on a sandwich.

Hondo sauntered closer and quipped, "Hillary and Heller, huh?" Taking a huge bite, he chewed and swallowed. He waved the remains of his sandwich, "So, Heller, do you ever get called 'Hell' for short?"

Eyes flashing, Heller retorted, "Don't be a fool. Of course not!"

"And what's with your clothes? Did you just come from a funeral?"

Hillary drew herself up and cast a haughty glare at Hondo. "This is the required attire for the Bradford Preparatory School of Dallas. It is an exclusive private academy for gifted and talented students."

"Yes, very exclusive," Heller added.

"But I wouldn't expect you to know about such things since you attend a public school." The twins glanced at each other with matching smirks.

Undaunted, Hondo stuffed the last of his sandwich in his mouth and brushed the crumbs off his shirt. "I guess it's going to be embarrassing then."

Heller looked at his sister. "Embarrassing?"

"Yes, what do you mean? What do we have anything to be embarrassed about?" Hillary demanded.

"I mean, what are you going to tell all the other rich kids when our *public* school kicks Bradford's butt and wins the robotics competition?"

Hillary and Heller stared at each other, then burst out laughing.

"Win? You must be joking!" Heller managed to say.

"You cobbled your robot together just three weeks ago. Win? Preposterous!" Hillary exclaimed.

"Don't know what 'preposterous' means, but I know our chances are as good or better than any of the other teams here."

Heller turned to Edison. "Surely you don't share this cretin's opinion that your team has any hope of winning"

"Surely not!" Hillary chimed in.

Edison glanced at Hondo. "We have a good robot and a good team. So, yes, I believe we can win."

"Bradford will win," Hillary sneered.

"We *always* win!" the twins finished.

An unspoken cue passed between them, and the twins spun on their heels and walked off.

"Wait!" Edison called after them. "How do you so much about me?"

The Breakstone's paused and faced Edison, cold smiles on their faces.

"We know everything about you, Edison Jones."

With that, they turned once again and melted into the crowd of students.

"Breakstone?" Edison mused. "The name sounds familiar for some reason."

Hondo took a long swig from his soft drink, then released an even longer belch. "I don't know what's weirder. That Hillary and Heller finish each other's sentences, or that there are two more geeks in the world who talk like you. I mean, what's a 'cretin' anyway?"

"Uh, trust me. You don't want to know," Edison replied. *Where have I heard the name Breakstone before?* His thoughts were interrupted when Carly and Bree swept into the room followed by a crowd of boys who soon swamped the cheerleader. Rather than get jostled in the competition for space next to her, Bree shook her head and joined Edison and Hondo.

"So, what have you two been up to?" she asked.

"Other than a visit by the Addams Family twins, nothing much," Hondo quipped.

"What do you mean? What happened?" Bree demanded.

Edison explained the sudden appearance of Hillary and Heller Breakstone, how they questioned him about his antigravity electromagnet, and how they seemed to know quite a bit about him.

"They even knew we just started on our robotics project three weeks ago. How could they know that unless—"

"Unless they were spying on you!" Bree finished for him.

The three friends cast uneasy glances at one another, and no one spoke for several moments. Finally, Hondo said, "C'mon, let's get out of here. It's become nerd central."

Bree shot him a withering look, and he raised his hands. "Whoa. No offense!"

Edison said, "Good idea. I want to Google the name Breakstone. I know I've heard the name before."

Markie stood unnoticed in a corner of the crowded room.

He followed with keen interest the entire conversation between the Breakstone twins and Edison. Although he heard very little of it in the noisy room, he had overheard enough, and he could tell by their facial expressions something was up.

A predatory smile appeared on his face, and he tossed his untouched plate of food into the nearest trash.

He headed off after Hillary and Heller.

CHAPTER 29

When Edison, Hondo, and Bree reached the relative quiet of the hotel lobby, Edison pulled a tablet from his backpack, and booted it up. He Googled the name, Breakstone. After a few moments of surfing, his breath caught in his throat and his face went white.

"It—it's them!"

"What? Who are you talking about?" Hondo demanded.

Bree placed her hand on Edison's shoulder. "Are you okay? Your face. It's all twisted."

"The Breakstone twins. *Their family killed my parents!*"

Stunned silence followed Edison's pronouncement. Hondo's mouth dropped open, while Bree chewed on her lip. She glanced back and forth between Edison and Hondo.

Carly skipped up. "Hey! What's going on? Why are you giving each other funny looks?" she chirped.

Hondo looked around. "Not here!" he warned. "Don't say anything until we get up to our room. C'mon!" Hondo led the way to the elevator. Edison, face ashen, followed with the girls close behind.

As they entered the lift, and Carly opened her mouth to speak. Hondo chopped his hand, and she clamped her jaws shut.

They rode to their floor in silence.

Sliding his key card into the slot, Hondo opened the door and motioned everyone into the room. He poked his head out into the hallway, looked both ways to make sure they weren't followed, then shut the door and locked it.

Carly threw up her hands. "Will someone please tell me what's going on?"

Hondo motioned to Edison. "You want to tell them or do you want me to?"

Edison took a few deep breaths to steady himself. "No. I'll do it." He then explained how his parents had been killed in a suspicious car accident. One thought to be deliberately staged by a rival technology company in an attempt to kill his grandfather—the same accident which left him in a wheelchair.

"But what do these twins have to do with your parents' death?" Bree asked.

"Hillary and Heller's family founded Breakstone Industries, which is the company we believe arranged the accident."

Bree gasped and Carly's eyes grew wide.

Knuckles white from clutching the arms of his anti-grav chair, Edison eased his grip and tried to reign in his emotions.

"Edison, I'm so sorry," Bree said.

Carly leaned over and hugged him. "We didn't know." Bree knelt beside Edison and covered his hand with hers.

Carly's faint perfume and Bree's warm touch left Edison's thoughts more jumbled than ever.

"Not many people know what I just told you. It's not like I try to keep it a big secret, it's just that it's hard…"

Emotion constricted his throat and Edison couldn't continue.

"It's difficult to talk about," Bree finished for him. She softly squeezed his arm. "We understand." Even through the shock of coming face-to-face with the Breakstones, Edison marveled at Bree's uncanny ability to read his emotions and connect with them.

Edison cleared his throat and managed to croak, "Thanks, Bree." With a deep breath, he tried to clear his mind. There was something he needed to do right away.

"I've got to let Grandpa and Carney know," he announced. He enabled the skype function on the tablet and moments later, a split screen image, one of his grandfather, the other of Carney, appeared.

Edison got right to the point. "I just met the Breakstone twins." He summarized how they ran into the brother and sister at the hospitality room, and how they seemed to know everything about him, particularly his anti-gravity elevator and even Team Edison's robotics project.

Stanton Jones nodded, a grim look on his face. "That explains the conference call I recently concluded with NASA. Apparently our good friend, Cutter Gentry, convinced his superiors more tests are needed before they certify the space elevator as a viable launch option."

Edison's nostrils flared. "What? That's crazy!"

"Oh, it gets better. Gentry managed to involve the EPA as well. They are demanding an environmental impact statement on any damaging effects the anti-gravity elevator might have on the ozone layer."

"The process is completely clean! There's no rocket fuel, gases, or any other propellant used in the anti-gravity process. Why would the EPA make such a request if they knew that?"

Disgusted, Stanton Jones growled, "Politics. I have my own contacts at NASA, and they tell me Breakstone Industries has their own version of a space elevator in development. Any company that can deliver payloads into space in a safe and inexpensive way stands to make a great deal of money."

He flashed Edison a grim look. "So you see, this is all about money. Breakstone Industries need time to complete their own launch project and beat us to the punch. Slowing down our certification provides them all the time they need."

"But that's not fair!" Hondo blurted.

Stanton Jones shook his head. "You're right. It's not fair. Unfortunately, money buys influence, and the Breakstone's have managed to spread a lot of it around to elected officials and highly placed individuals in government agencies. I have no doubt Gentry's hand is deep into Breakstone Industries' pocket."

Anger glinted in Jones's eyes. "But I can play this game too. In the meantime, we will comply with any government agency's request."

Edison fumed and gritted his teeth. "Okay, Grandpa. I know you will do whatever you can."

"What do you want me to do, Sir?" Carney asked. Although he had kept his silence throughout the conversation, Edison could tell from the thrust of his jaw and the thin line of his lips, the news did not sit well with him.

"I want you in Dallas with Edison—the sooner, the better. Bring all the personnel you need to keep an eye on Edison *and* the Breakstones! There are too many coincidences here, and it worries me they know so much about Edison and what he is involved in. We may have a mole in our own company."

"Understood. I'll take a LogicTech jet and be in Dallas within the hour." Carney's image blinked out.

Stanton Jones returned his attention to Edison. "Be careful! I don't know what the Breakstone's are up to, but it's bound to be no good. Simple curiosity about your anti-gravity elevator seems too farfetched given what we know of their business concerns. So, under no circumstances are you to go anywhere alone, particularly until Carney arrives at your hotel. I'm going to do some more digging, and when I arrive later tonight, we can talk about this further."

"I'll stay with Edison, Mr. Jones," Hondo declared. "Anywhere he goes, I'll go."

"We'll be with him too!" Bree added with Carly at her shoulder.

For the first time, Stanton Jones smiled. "Looks like you're in good hands. Call me at once if anything else comes up." Jones' image winked out.

Edison released a long sigh. What started that morning as a trip to the regional robotics competition, now suddenly turned into something far more complicated. He couldn't begin to guess what the Breakstone twins were up to.

Hondo pounded a large fist into the palm of his hand as if prepared to throw a punch at the first person to walk through the door. Bree and Carly hovered next to him, never more than an arm's length away. His friends were worried about him.

His friends.

Edison couldn't help himself. He grinned. *No matter what, we can do anything together!*

A charge of adrenaline coursed through him, and Edison activated the tablet's touchscreen.

We have a robotics competition to prepare for!

CHAPTER 30

The rest of the evening went by uneventfully.

As promised, Carney arrived at the hotel thirty minutes later. A number of LogicTech security personnel arrived with him, and quickly spread throughout the hotel. Well trained, they blended in with the other hotel occupants.

Edison's grandfather arrived later that night. He had discovered nothing new other than confirmation Breakstone Industries was indeed behind NASA's roadblock to Edison's space elevator.

Carney's men reported no sign of Hillary and Heller Breakstone—it was if they had disappeared. Rather than reassure Edison, the news only served to deepen his worry.

What are they up to?

He spent a restless night tossing and turning. When Mr. Russell knocked on their door early the next morning, he felt relieved for an excuse to finally get out of bed. One glance at Hondo, rubbing red eyes as he opened the door, indicated his friend also endured a uneasy night.

Cheerful, Mr. Russell stepped inside and rubbed his hands briskly. "Breakfast is at 7:30, then we'll meet in the lobby at 8:30. I'll have the van out front, and we'll drive straight to the Convention Center. The first round of the competition starts at 9:00 sharp with our robot slated to compete at 9:45. Any questions about the schedule?"

Edison managed to pull himself out of bed and into his hoverchair, yawned, and shook his head. His eyes widened when he noticed Markie behind the science teacher in the hallway. The big boy wore a smug expression, and when Mr. Russell turned to leave, a smile spread across his face.

He spun and followed Mr. Russell.

A cold chill crawled up Edison's spine. *That's creepy. He acts like he knows something we don't.*

"Did you notice anything different about Markie?" Edison asked Hondo.

Hondo stretched and yawned. "Other than he still has the same butt-ugly face? No. Why?"

"I don't know. Maybe coming face-to-face with those creepy Breakstone twins has me imagining things. I just thought Markie looked kind of weird. Like he knew a secret or something."

"Franks? Well, in my imagination, I have my fist pushed up his nose, but then you have your dreams and I have mine."

Edison laughed, the tension slipping off his shoulders. "Yeah, I guess I'm too sensitive."

Hondo grinned. "That's more like it! C'mon, let's get ready. I'm starved!"

Forty-five minutes later, showered and dressed, the boys made their way to the breakfast buffet. Carney met them at the elevator and followed them to breakfast. Carly and Bree, already at a table, motioned for Edison and Hondo to join them. Edison barely placed his tray on the table when the girls peppered him with questions.

"Have you heard anything else?"

"Yes, what did your grandfather say?"

Edison shrugged. "Not much, other than to confirm Breakstone Industries is behind the slowdown to certify my space elevator." He paused and scanned the room. "Any of you see Markie?"

Bree shrugged. "He was in here earlier with Mr. Russell. Why?"

"Oh, nothing. Just curious."

Hondo waved a slice of bacon. "Hey, are you trying to ruin my appetite?"

Edison managed a grin. "Sorry." He picked at his food.

The sense of foreboding refused to go away.

"Good luck!" Mr. Russell said to Edison and the rest of the robotics team.

They stood on the convention floor next to a half-dozen pits or caged areas where the robots would compete. Only the student teams were allowed on the floor. Sponsors, family members, and other spectators watched from the temporary stands on either side of the pit.

"You'll do fine. We're proud of all of you," Stanton Jones added as he and Carney turned and followed the science teacher.

Raucous cheers and shouts of support reverberated off the walls of the spacious arena while Edison and his crew prepped their 'bot. The competition was already underway, with hundreds of engineering teams from across the state along with thousands of spectators, packed into the convention center. The stands shook with applause every time a robot successfully put a ball through a basketball hoop set up in each cage.

"You ready?" Edison asked Hondo who kept wiping his hands on his shirt.

"I guess I'm as ready as I'll ever be. Even football never gave me the shakes like this," Hondo admitted.

"Hey, you'll do fine!" Edison assured his friend.

A roar arose from the crowd at another successful shot.

Hondo grimaced. "I hope you're right."

A voice cut through the crowd noise. "What? Edwards screw up? That would *never* happen! My money's on you, Edwards."

Hondo's eyes narrowed. Markie lounged in a chair next to the staging area, a smirk on his face. Edison clamped a hand on his friend's arm as he stepped toward the bully.

"It's okay," Hondo said, shaking off Edison's hand. "Nothing's going to happen."

He walked over to Markie's chair, stopped, and looked down at him. "Franks, despite your lazy ass, we managed to finish the project. On the few occasions you actually showed up to help, you spent most of your time throwing a ball against a wall."

He squatted to eye level with Markie. "But I don't care because you stayed out of the way." Hondo leaned closer. "So, that's all you have to do now, Franks. Just stay out of the way."

Markie held Hondo's gaze for a few moments. Then a sly smile appeared on his lips. "Oh, you can count on that, Edwards. I'll be happy to let you and the other grunts do all the work."

Unsure what to do next in the tense atmosphere, Edison shifted nervously in the hoverchair.

He almost jumped out of his skin when a lanky man shouted, "Harpersville," and broke up the staring match. "You're up next!"

An official's badge hung from a lanyard around the man's neck, and he waved them toward a gate entrance into one of the caged pits.

Using the remote, Edison powered up the robot, and it trundled toward the gate. The rest of Team Edison followed close behind.

The official pointed to a large digital monitor mounted above the cage. "You have five minutes to prep. Once the clock counts down to zero, you have thirty seconds to engage the autonomous phase of your robot's programming. When the buzzer goes off, your fifteen seconds of independent operation begins. At the end of the autonomous process, a ten second delay will occur. Then ninety seconds of operator control begins. Any questions?"

The team members shook their heads.

"Right. Good luck then."

He nodded at an official timekeeper seated behind a table, and the digital countdown started.

Edison eyed the monitor, their robot positioned by the open gate leading into the pit. Finger poised above the engage key on the remote, when the countdown reached zero, he hit the key and the robot immediately moved toward the ball bin. Smoothly, its articulated arms scooped up balls and began to shoot at the nine foot goal.

The first two shots went in.

Carly and Bree cheered wildly as the robot, without pause, continued to pick up balls and shoot. When the buzzer went off, seven shots had been made for a total of twenty-one points.

The official whistled. "Congratulations. That's one of the highest autonomous scores so far. Are you ready for the operator control phase?"

Grinning, Edison handed the remote to Hondo. "Yes, we're ready."

Hondo's hands shook as he took the remote. Edison patted him on the arm. "Don't worry. You've done this a million times." His big friend took a deep breath, a glint of determination in his eyes.

He turned to face the robot. "Let's do this!"

CHAPTER 31

Gaze glued to the countdown on the monitor, Hondo cracked his knuckles. When the buzzer sounded his fingers attacked the remote.

Smoothly, the robot trundled to the ball bin. Once in position, Hondo had its arms digging balls out. He made a test shot, then waited before tossing another ball at the goal.

It clanked off the top of the backboard, well off the mark.

Hondo quickly made adjustments on the control console, then released a second ball. It missed also, but this time the shot rimmed in and out.

Now with less than sixty seconds left, Hondo made more corrections. He shoveled up a ball and directed the robot to shoot.

The ball went down into the cylinder…then rolled out!

Even above the crowd noise, Hondo heard the groans from Carly and Bree. Jaw clenched, he fine-tuned his adjustments. In the back of his mind, he tried to recall the training sessions. Edison told him the act of shooting a ball was a practice in physics…something about force and mass multiplied by acceleration. Now he wished he paid more attention, but it still came down to one simple fact.

Put the ball in the hoop!

With forty-five seconds left, Hondo directed the 'bot to grab two more balls. He let one fly and held his breath.

It went in! Grinning, Hondo immediately released the second shot and it swished through the hoop. *Take that! I got the range.*

"Yes!"

Out of the corner of his eye, he caught sight of the girls jumping up and down and cheering madly. A glance at the monitor told him only thirty seconds remained.

He chortled. *More than enough time!*

The remote's control console contained a special red key—one which Hondo carefully avoided touching. One of Edison's adaptations to the robot's CRIO or brain had been to add what he called range memory. Since every CRIO was identical with the same memory capacity, each team had to be careful with their programming. If the coding ran past the data capacity, it would freeze the program and lock-up the robot.

Edison called it information overload—a concept Hondo experienced every time he set foot in a classroom. However, Edison's genius was to plug in bytes of software which boosted the CRIO's potential without blowing up its memory. This allowed their robot to remember its exact position and the force times acceleration stuff key to each successful attempt.

Hondo hit the red button.

Retrieving two balls out of the bin, the robot released them one at a time. Both shots went in, barely rippling the net. With glee, Hondo punched the red key again and again. When the buzzer went off, he jerked his eyes to the scoreboard.

Ten shots!

"Outstanding! Absolutely remarkable!" Rick, the robotics official, exclaimed. "Congratulations, Harpersville. Your combined point total is fifty-one. That's one of the highest first day point totals I've ever seen!"

Team Edison celebrated with hugs and high-fives. In the stands, Mr. Russell pumped his fist while Carney whistled and pounded him on the back. Edison's grandfather showed more reserve, but still wore a wide smile and clapped enthusiastically.

Elated, Edison sat back in his hoverchair while his friends continued to celebrate. Arms crossed, Markie stood nearby, looking like he just swallowed a sour lemon.

Edison dismissed Markie's reaction as more of the same lack of enthusiasm he had exhibited all along.

I'm not going to let it ruin one of the best days of my life.

Edison clenched his tablet and waved it high above his head. "Yes!" he shouted.

Stanton Jones had treated the entire team to lunch at a nearby Fuddruckers, including Mr. Russell. Seated around a table, they replayed the high points of Team Edison's victory. Markie chose to be the only member not present, claiming he had an upset stomach.

Hondo looked up from the hamburger he was wolfing down. "What?" he asked around a mouthful of burger.

"We made the second round finals with the most points of any team!"

Another round of celebration exploded and heads swiveled all over the restaurant at the commotion. Stanton Jones waved his hands for calm.

Mr. Russell, caught up in the boisterous celebration, said, "S-sorry. I've never had a team make it to the second round before…much less be leading in points."

"I think you can be excused," Jones said chuckling. "It's quite an accomplishment."

Having finally demolished his burger, Hondo asked, "Who else made the finals?"

Edison returned his attention to the tablet. "Let's see." He called up the results and scrolled through the them. Seconds later, a grim look appeared on his face.

"Austin Westlake's team is in third," Edison relayed. He shook his head. "Bradford Preparatory School is in second, three points behind us."

"I'd like to have seen Hillary and Heller's face when they found out they came in second," Hondo snickered.

"It's only the opening round of the competition," Edison warned. "The final round is what counts."

"So what? We'll beat'em again, and you know why?"

Hondo jumped up and stood next to Edison, a huge grin plastered across his face. "Because we have Edison Jones!"

Hondo grabbed Edison's arm and raised it high in the air. He danced around the hoverchair like he just scored a touchdown. His friend's enthusiasm soon had everyone cheering anew. Heads, once again, turned to see what the uproar was all about. Although uncomfortable with all the attention, Edison couldn't stop the smile which spread across his face.

Soon it was as wide as Hondo's.

CHAPTER 32

EDISON LAY IN BED, UNABLE TO SLEEP. WITH ARMS CLASPED BEHIND his head, he replayed the day's events in his mind.

Mr. Russell insisted they all turn in early—which Stanton Jones heartily seconded—so they returned to the hotel shortly after finishing their meal. Unable to sleep, Edison dissected, step-by-step, their 'bot's performance. In the midst of his analysis, Hondo's voice cut through the dark.

"I'm sorry about your parents, Edison."

Startled, Edison fumbled for a reply. "Uh, that's okay. Thanks."

Since the day in his underground lab when Edison shared the story of his parent's murder, they talked very little about the sensitive incident.

"I never knew my old man," Hondo continued. "Mama used to have a picture of him on the refrigerator under a magnet. I'd see his face every time I opened the fridge. One night, Mama came home drunk, and the next day, his picture was gone."

Edison remained silent. Hondo, normally close-mouthed about his family, always acted like he would rather talk about anything but them.

"I don't think I'd recognize my old man if he walked up to me tomorrow. Not that we would have much to talk about since he never bothered to call or even send me a birthday card."

Uncertain why Hondo brought up the subject of his parents, Edison turned his head and strained to see Hondo's face in the darkened room.

"I guess I just want to know what it's like."

Unable to restrain himself any longer, Edison blurted, "What do you mean?"

"You know. To have a *real* mom or a *real* dad."

Speechless, Edison heard Hondo turn over in his bed. A few moments later, soft snores filled the heavy silence.

Edison lay back and stared at the ceiling. His mind did a quick reverse course from analysis of their robot's performance. *Why did Hondo, all of a sudden, start to talk about his family?*

He was tempted to slip out of bed, get in his anti-grav chair, and go knock on Bree and Carly's door. Bree seemed to have an uncanny perception of these things. Surely she could help him understand. But, it was late, they would already be in bed, and of course, Carly would demand to know why Edison wanted to talk to Bree.

Frustrated, Edison mulled it over. The thoughts of his own parents started to surface. Smiling, he recalled how his father would lift him onto his shoulders when he got home from work. While they would marched around the house, Edison, on his lofty perch, chattered away. Sometimes, his father would tickle his foot until he squirmed and laughed uncontrollably. No matter how much Edison kicked and wriggled, however, his father never lost his grip, nor did Edison ever worry he would be dropped.

He always felt safe. He always felt loved.

And then, like an electric shock, it hit him.

Maybe that's what Hondo meant about having a real mother and father.

Not a day passed that he didn't miss his own parents. He would give anything to see their faces just once more—to feel his mother's hug or hear his father's laugh. Edison's eyes welled with tears, and he grabbed the edge of the bed sheet to wipe them.

Edison turned but he could barely see Hondo's dim silhouette form in the murky darkness. However brief, he at least had known a parent's love, and of course, Grandpa loved him. Hondo would never have that experience, either.

A sadness for his friend settled like a leaden weight on him. A new understanding of what life must be like for Hondo grew within his mind and heart. With a sigh, Edison closed his eyes, but before he fell asleep, he made a mental promise.

I'll never feel sorry for myself again.

After breakfast, they arrived early at the convention center. Already filled with teams and spectators, the place buzzed with activity for the second and final day of competition.

The Westlake and Bradford teams were also there putting their robots through their paces. Edison did a final diagnostic check and proclaimed they were ready to go. Since Team Edison scored the most points, they would go last.

Westlake went first. Their robot performed well, but they were unable to increase their point total from the forty-five points scored the first day.

Bradford Preparatory went next.

Hillary and Heller smirked as they walked by Edison's team. Other Bradford members, clad in the same black blazers, followed with noses held high.

Hondo remarked, "They all act like they have corn cobs up their—"

"*Shhh!*" Bree scolded.

Hondo grinned and held up his hands. "Just sayin'."

The Bradford robot, a flat black with the Bradford insignia embossed on its metal frame, trundled into the pit. It performed the autonomous phase with flawless perfection. Heller then took the controls and directed the automaton's actions in the operator controlled phase. After a few near misses, shot after shot swished through the hoop. When the buzzer sounded, all eyes darted to the scoreboard.

A roar swelled and rippled through the audience. Bradford scored fifty-two points.

One better than Team Edison's total the previous day.

Edison gulped. Bradford's total would be hard to beat. Their robot would have to be almost perfect in both phases of the competition.

"Harpersville! You're up," an official called out.

Edison directed their robot to the pit, the other project members crowding around him. Markie stood back with a wide smile. It seemed strange to Edison, but he didn't have time to think about it. The countdown clock had run to zero.

He gripped the controller and engaged the autonomous stage.

Nothing happened.

Edison hit the key again with the same result. He quickly checked the power level.

Fully charged.

Repeated attempts all ended in failure. Their robot remained motionless.

Edison raised his hand. "Time!" he called.

The official immediately raised his own hand and said, "Harpersville has called time. The clock has been reset for five minutes." The digital clock began to count down.

Edison backed their robot out of the pit. He examined it with the other project members huddled beside him.

"The rules state we have five minutes to fix the problem. After that, we're out."

"What's wrong?" Hondo asked.

"Don't know," Edison replied. "It worked perfectly when I ran a final systems check."

He reached and pulled the CRIO out. He pressed a button and a wafer-thin section popped out. His eyes widened.

"It's gone!"

Edison looked up. "The memory card is gone. All our coding is on it. Without the chip, the robot is blind. It doesn't know what to do."

Hondo stiffened. "Wait a minute. Where's Markie?"

The team members looked up. Markie leaned against one of the support stanchions. He held up a hand. One-by-one, he closed his digits until only one remained.

The middle finger.

He turned and disappeared into the crowd.

CHAPTER 33

EDISON GRABBED HONDO'S ARM AS HE STARTED AFTER MARKIE.

"Lemme go. He's probably got the memory card on him, and I'm going to get it!"

"Hondo, no! By the time you catch him, *if* you catch him, our five minutes will be up and we'll be disqualified."

His big friend threw his arms up. "So what are we going to do? You got an extra CRIO up your sleeve? Because if you don't, we'll be disqualified anyway."

Edison's thoughts raced. *All the hours we practiced putting our robot through its paces, the time Hondo spent adjusting its trajectory until every shot went in. Now, Markie short circuited all our hard work—*

"Wait! The rules allow us to skip the autonomous stage and use yesterday's score."

Hondo shook his head. "What good does that do? Bradford is ahead of us now. Unless we improve our own score, they win."

Edison tapped Hondo's arm. "What do you do every day after school?"

Hondo shrugged. "I practice football. What does—"

"Muscle memory! You call it practice, but whenever you execute a play or throw a pass, what you are really doing is an exercise in neural repetition."

Hondo frowned. "I don't know what—"

His eyes widened. "Oh, no. You must be crazy. There's no way I can go into that pit and come close to making a shot without the CRIO."

Edison scooted his anti-grav chair closer. "Look, we skip the autonomous stage, and go straight to the operator's phase. You've practiced it a hundred times already. You just need to do it once more."

"I tell you it won't work!"

Edison sat back and crossed his arms. "If this was a football field and our robot a receiver, how many attempts would you need to hit him with a twenty-yard pass? How about a thirty-yard pass?"

Hondo waved a hand. "Once. I could do it with my eyes closed."

"See? How is it any different with our robot."

Hondo opened his mouth...then closed it.

Edison leaned closer to his friend. "All you have to do is find the range. Once you've done that, the rest is easy. Just make sure you lock in the setting and shoot away just like you've done a hundred times. It's the only chance to increase our score."

Hondo scratched his chin. "I don't know."

Carly moved closer and looped her arm through his. Both she and Bree had followed the exchange closely. She stood on her toes and tapped his head. "You can do it," she said. "There's so much more to you than just football. Believe in yourself like I do—I mean like we do—and you'll be amazed what you can accomplish."

Edison's mouth dropped. Carly, the bubbly, effervescent girl with the mile-a-minute mouth, had transformed chameleon-like to a maturity level he never would have believed.

He shook his head. *Which is the real Carly?*

Bree interrupted his thoughts. "No matter what happens, we've won," she said to Hondo. "You get your project grade and pass science, and Harpersville's robot advances farther than any project in school history. Markie can't take that away."

Hondo nodded. "Okay." He slammed his fist in the palm of his hand. "I can't wait to see the Breakstone twin's faces when we beat them."

"Times up!" the clock official cried. "Harpersville, are you ready?"

Hondo grabbed the controller from Edison.

"Let's go!"

The digital clock counted down, 3, 2, 1…

When the buzzer went off, Hondo already had the robot on the move. Wheels trundling, he steered it into the pit.

He positioned their automaton so its arms faced the hoop and net. The first two shots were badly off the mark. A trickle of sweat rolled down his forehead.

'Muscle memory', Edison said. A chuckle escaped his lips.

That means don't think, and I do "don't think" better than anybody!

Hondo relaxed and let his reflexes take over. The next shot bounced off the back of the goal, with the follow-up shot rimming in and out. Each time he made minute adjustments.

Swish.

He sank the shot with barely a ripple. A fierce smile stretched from ear-to-ear. *I've found the range.*

He locked the robot in place and checked the time.

One minute left.

Shot after shot rose from the automaton. Articulated arms scooped up one ball after another.

Without a single miss.

The buzzer blared. Hondo's fists pumped the air at the final score. *Sixty-two points.*

Ten more than Bradford Prep.

Edison joined the wild celebration. The members of Team Edison shouted and bounced up and down on their toes when the head official declared Harpersville the official winner.

Edison sucked in a breath at the sight of Hondo, the controller high over his head, acting like he was going to spike it like a football. "No!" he cried.

His big friend pointed at him. "Gotcha."

Edison laughed and Hondo sidled closer. "Besides, I need this in one piece when I shove it up Markie's butt."

Edison's jaw dropped. "Gotcha again," Hondo cried and danced away to pick up Carly and hug her.

Two familiar figures clad in black blazers approached. The team members looked up warily, and Hondo moved to stand next to Edison

"Congratulations," Hillary and Heller said in unison, the tepid compliment reeking with a lack of warmth and enthusiasm.

"Looks like the plan you cooked up with Markie didn't work out so well, did it?" Hondo smirked.

The twin's ignored him, their attention focused on Edison.

"We propose another competition, one not so juvenile as this," said Heller.

"Yes, one in which the winner gets far more than a pat on the back and a dusty trophy," added Hillary.

Edison's eyes narrowed. "We won. Why should we have another competition? Besides the school won't—"

"This has nothing to do with the school. This would be a private affair," Hillary interjected.

"Two armored robots—yours and ours—would face off against each other. The survivor is the winner. I believe your childish friends here call them 'Combat Bots'," Heller added.

Edison shook his head. "I don't think so. We've got better things to do."

Heller glanced at his sister, a gleam in his eye. "I understand your space elevator has run into regulatory problems. Such a shame after so much time and work has gone into it."

Hillary picked at a piece of nonexistent lint on her blazer. "Our father has connections. It's possible he could use his considerable influence to have your anti-gravity elevator approved if your robot wins."

Edison sat up, lips in a tight line. "And if we lose?"

"Then you agree to cease development of the space elevator for a period of ten years," Heller answered. "And Breakstone Industries will usher in a new age of launch technology." The twins shared a twisted smile.

"Not you, Edison Jones," they said in unison.

CHAPTER 34

"BLACKMAIL. THE BREAKSTONE'S ARE BLACKMAILING ME!"

Edison fumed and stared stonily at his friends. Now gathered in his lab, Team Edison's victory was muted by Hillary and Heller's 'bot challenge. The trip back to Harpersville, rather than happy and energetic, was completed in strained silence.

And no one saw Markie again.

Mr. Russell told them his mother called to say an uncle would pick him up and take him home. Although glad for that bit of good news—Edison didn't want to think what might happen if Hondo laid eyes on him any time soon—it did little to distract his attention from the twins' proposal.

It's all he thought about on the long drive home.

"Shouldn't you tell your grandfather?" Bree asked. "Isn't this proof of a conspiracy to block your space elevator?"

Edison shook his head. "It wouldn't make any difference. It would be their word against mine. Grandpa already has an army of lawyers trying to get it approved. Besides, if I told him, he might try to stop me from accepting the Breakstone's challenge. I'm going to wait until I've got the combat 'bot fabricated and functional. Then it will be harder for him to say no."

Hondo jerked his head toward Edison. "Wait a minute. You aren't going to agree to this crazy competition, are you?"

Edison shrugged. "I don't have any choice."

"They're lying cheats! They already got Markie to sabotage our robot. No telling what those creepy twins will do next."

Bree put her hand on Edison's shoulder. "I agree with Hondo."

"You can't trust them," Carly chimed in.

Edison scratched his chin. "They'll *try* to cheat. However, there may be a way we can use that against them."

Hondo stared. "Huh? What do you mean?"

"If we are convinced the twins will do something underhanded, then it becomes a factor, and as a factor, we can plug it into the equation just like any problem. From this we can create a solution which uses the twin's own character against them."

"Oh, no. Not again," Hondo groaned. "Do you really think any of us understand what you just said?"

Bree raised her hand. "I do."

"Oh, sure. One brainiac to another." Hondo threw his arms up. "Why am I not surprised?"

Carly cleared her throat. "What Edison means is he can use the twins own nature against them. In fact, I think he's counting on the Breakstone's attempt to cheat."

Hondo's jaw fell open, and Edison grinned at his friend's reaction. Although Carly continued to surprise him, Hondo looked like a feather could knock him down.

"Uh, yes. You're right," Edison said.

Edison leaned forward. "I've got an idea for our 'bot I don't think the Breakstones could ever prepare for.

"Here's what I have in mind..."

Edison punched a key and the monitor chirped once, twice, and then resolved to show Hillary and Heller standing shoulder-to-shoulder smirking.

"Edison Jones! Have you considered our proposal?"

Edison nodded. "I have." He turned and motioned at his friends beside him. "We accept. What are the rules?"

Hillary and Heller looked at each other, sneers widening. Hillary spoke first. "We follow the same guidelines and limitations from the recent automaton competition with the following changes."

Heller took up the narrative. "First, the CRIO's memory has no restrictions. Second, the combat robot's functions are entirely autonomous, with no operator control. Third, there is no time limit, the competition ends when only one functioning automaton remains."

"In order to be declared the winner," Hillary continued, "the robot must be able to leave the battle cage under its own power. If neither automaton is able to accomplish this, a draw will be called."

The twins' gaze narrowed at Edison. "In two weeks, we will meet in a hangar at a private airfield owned by Breakstone Industries," they spoke in unison. "We will carry out the competition there."

The connection ended, and Breakstone's' image winked out.

"What? No teary goodbye?" Hondo quipped.

Edison didn't respond, his brow creased in thought.

Bree, worried at Edison's silence, asked, "Is something wrong?"

Edison bit his lip. "I think the cheating we talked about has already started."

At his friend's blank expressions, Edison rotated his anti-grav chair to face them. "They gave us only two weeks in order to squeeze us for time. I'm sure their 'bot is ready to go. Then, they picked the location, one owned by Breakstone Industries. They're on familiar territory, while we will have to mock up our own cage to practice in. Besides, there's no telling how many sensors and digital devices they could have planted in and around the battle cage."

Hondo scratched his head. "Doesn't sound like your *factor* is going to be as easy as you thought."

A smile grew on Edison's face. "Actually everything is going according to plan.

"Just the way I thought it would."

Hondo lounged beside a kiosk littered with wires and other electrical components. Edison and Bree were hunched over his computer, their attention on the monitor. Carly walked over to stand beside Hondo.

"I didn't know you were so good at foreign languages," he said.

Carly cocked her head. "I don't know any foreign language. I'm barely passing Intro to Spanish."

"Well, you understand Edison-Speak real good."

"Oh, that," Carly laughed. She waved a hand. "I have my moments."

Hondo scratched his chin. "Yeah. I guess there's more to you than I thought."

"I hope so." Carly fidgeted then crossed her arms. "I'm glad you noticed. Sometimes, I wonder if you even know I'm there."

She spun and hurried over to join Edison and Bree.

Hondo's mouth fell open. Carly glanced back at him once, then quickly turned away.

An odd feeling wormed its way inside him. He had known Carly since the fifth grade, and she had been a constant presence ever since, whether in class or cheering from the sideline. Until now, he just took her for granted—like a kid sister who always hung around.

But now she seemed different.

Maybe it's time to notice her a little more.

CHAPTER 35

"WOULD YOU SETTLE DOWN?" EDISON HUFFED.

Seated in the cafeteria, Edison shook his head while Hondo alternated between twirling a football in his hands and attacking the food on his tray.

Toss the ball in the air.

Catch.

Grab a bite of a corny dog.

Repeat.

Edison pushed his own tray away. "I can't eat. I'm afraid you're going to miss and drop the football in my salad."

Hondo snorted. "As if. Besides, it might improve your rabbit food."

Edison shrugged. "Leafy vegetables are good for you. When combined with nuts and fruits, they are loaded with antioxidants—"

"The big game's tonight, Edison! You think I care about—"

Edison's grin stopped Hondo's rant. His big friend chuckled and pointed the football at him. "For someone with nothing but computers for friends the past five years, you're getting pretty good at kiddin' around."

Edison's smile grew wider. "Well, I guess I've had good teachers."

"You sure have. Me!" Hondo stood up and bowed. "I need to start charging you by the hour."

Edison forked some lettuce. "At least I've gotten your mind on something else."

Hondo sat down and tucked the football under his arm. He leaned forward. "Coach said no junior high team has ever beaten Paris since he's been at Harpersville…we'd be the first!"

"I think you will—"

Edison's face fell at the sight of Markie Franks headed for their table.

Members of his gang trailed behind him like cows following a herd bull. He stopped and dropped his tray with a loud clatter several feet from where they sat. Soon the once empty table became filled with Markie and his followers.

"Heard we have a football game tonight," he said to his throng. "I can't decide if I want to go or not. 'Course, we'll probably lose since we have such a pussy for a quarterback, but then, it might be fun to see the ass-whupping." Laughter erupted all around.

Edison's heart sank. He started to reach for Hondo then stopped. The violent reaction he expected never materialized. Instead, Hondo resumed tossing the football, a smile on his face.

"I think you should come, Franks. You're gonna see history made tonight." He caught the ball, put it aside, then placed both hands on the table.

"But, the quarterback's not going to win the game. The *team* is. You know what a team is don't you, Franks? Like the robotics team you tried to mess up?"

Markie's face turned dark.

Hondo stood. "We've got a great team. That's why we'll win." He waved his arm at Markie's gang. "You, on the other hand, are stuck with these losers."

With a wink, he added, "Along with those cute little boxers you like to wear."

Markie's cheeks now took on the color of a ripe plum.

"C'mon, Edison. It stinks like something rotten in here." Hondo turned and made his way for the exit.

Edison swiveled his anti-grav chair, and in so doing, caught sight of Markie's gaze following Hondo's every step.

His face twisted with hatred.

The crowd roared as the Harpersville team took to the field.

With his digital cam already airborne, Edison turned toward the stands. Full to bursting, he didn't spot an empty seat. Fans spilled outside the perimeter fence surrounding the football field. Many brought lawn chairs and claimed choice spots from which to view the game through the fence.

It looks like half the town's population turned out...and for a junior high game!

The energy sizzled and even Edison felt himself caught up in it. When Harpersville kicked off to Paris, he joined in the wild cheering.

It didn't take long for Edison to realize this game wouldn't be like the others played by the seventh-grade team. Paris' players were big, strong, and fast. Hondo—as a two-way player on both the offense and defense—normally made plays from his linebacker position behind the line of scrimmage. Against Paris, he was forced to make tackles after gains of five to ten yards. Only a fumble recovered by Harpersville stopped the Wildcats from scoring on their first drive.

Once on offense, Hondo led the team methodically down the

field. Here again, Edison could see a clear difference. In other games, his big friend often ran for long plays because the smaller players couldn't tackle him. Now, he was punished with every running play, and no rushing attempt went for more than five or six yards.

On the Harpersville forty-nine yard-line, Hondo faked a hand-off to set up a play-action pass. Completely fooled, not a single Paris defender was within ten yards of the receiver as he streaked down the field. Hondo dropped back and lofted a pass just as two Wildcat defenders hit him. Perfectly thrown, the receiver never broke stride as he cradled the pass.

Touchdown.

The crowd roared, and the stands shook in celebration.

The rest of the half reflected the closeness of the game. At halftime, Harpersville led by a score of 7-6.

Drained, Edison sat back in his anti-grav chair. He shook his head. *There's another half to go!*

He checked on the video drone and replayed some of the footage. Everything seemed in order, so he turned his thoughts back to the game filled with kids his own age who could all run, jump, and tackle. They played a sport he could only dream about. In what was now a recurring theme, he wondered anew what it would be like to run and catch a pass.

He tried not to dwell on it, but he couldn't help the bitter shake of his head.

I can invent an anti-gravity elevator.
But I can't create a new set of legs.

The second half of the game proved to be just as closely contested. The two teams battled back and forth until Harpersville managed a field goal from the fifteen-yard line to make the score 10-6. Other than the lone field goal, both defenses dominated and neither team could mount a scoring drive.

Time ticked off the clock, and Harpersville took possession on a failed fourth down attempt by the Wildcats. On their own thirty-yard line, only two minutes remained in the game.

Hondo took the snap and handed off to the running back. Immediately met by a Wildcat defender, a crushing tackle separated the ball from the running back and it squirted down the field. Both teams pursued the loose ball until a Paris player fell on it.

The ball rested on the Harpersville eight-yard line.

First-and-goal-to-goal.

A minute and forty-five seconds to go.

The Harpersville defense trotted back onto the field, and a collective groan rose from the crowd.

The first play from scrimmage netted four yards. With no time outs left, Paris hurried another running play gaining only two yards. The ball now rested on the two-yard line.

On the next play, the Wildcat running back, hit at the line of scrimmage, still managed to lunge forward for another yard.

Fourth down, twenty seconds left, the ball on the one-yard line.

The screams from the fans filled the air to such an extent, Edison's hoverchair vibrated. He leaned forward, the anticipation almost unbearable.

The Wildcat quarterback received the snap, then took a step and launched himself into the air. He soared over the line of scrimmage where Hondo met him in midair.

With a *crunch*, Hondo drove the quarterback in the opposite direction for no gain. The horn blared to signal the game's end.

Harpersville had beaten the mighty Paris Wildcats.

CHAPTER 36

"You aren't coming to the dance?"

Edison shook his head. "No. I need to work on the battle robot."

Bree sat beside Edison in the school library. A stack of books lay on the table between them. She picked up one of the books, *Little Women*, and fingered the pages.

"Are you sure it isn't something else?"

Shifting in his hoverchair, Edison asked, "Uh, what do you mean?"

She put the book down and looked at him. "You know exactly what I mean."

Edison threw his hands up. "Okay, okay. Everyone will be dancing but me. Instead, I'll be in my usual seated position watching everyone else." He crossed his arms. "Satisfied?"

Scooting closer, Bree placed a hand on his shoulder. "Edison, a lot of kids don't dance either. They go to have fun, see their friends and have a good time. You can do the same thing."

"I'll still be the only one in this," Edison groused, and gripped the arms of the anti-grav chair so hard his knuckles turned white.

"Please, Edison," Bree pleaded. "I bought a new dress and I hoped—well, I hoped you would go with me."

Edison's mouth dropped. He turned to Bree, but she quickly looked away.

Bree picked up her books, and stood. "I'm sorry. I know how sensitive you can be, and I didn't mean to make you feel uncomfortable." She began to walk away.

"Wait!"

Bree stopped and Edison waved at her. "Come back. I didn't say no."

Tears glistened in her eyes. "It's okay. You don't have to—"

"I'll go."

Books still balanced in her arms, Bree asked, "But why? You just told me you didn't want to."

Edison grinned. "That was before I knew I would be going with you. You'll have to find other dance partners, though."

"Are you sure?" Hope sparkled in her eyes.

"Positive."

Bree sniffled and shuffled her feet. "Okay."

She took a step, then turned back. "I don't care about your wheelchair or whether you can walk or run. I care about *you*. Hondo, Carly, we all feel the same way. So if it doesn't matter to us, why should it matter to you?"

Bree checked out her books and left the library.

Her question hung in the air. Like a balloon, it floated before him, just out of reach.

Why does it matter? he repeated to himself. No one had ever posed his disability to him like that before.

The question followed him the rest of the day.

The dance was Friday night.

In the backseat, Edison's hands fluttered in his lap as Carney drove to Bree's house. The big ex-SEAL pulled up and parked the car, then leaned back and winked. "You're up."

Edison took a deep breath and held up a pink and white corsage. "You think Bree will like this?"

Carney chuckled. "No worries there. Girls always like flowers."

The anti-grav chair rose from the open trunk and hovered by the door. Edison pushed himself into the seat, smoothed his white, button-down shirt, and straightened the pleats on his khaki slacks. Then he made his way to the entrance of the brick home.

The door opened as he came to a stop. Bree stood on the threshold, a wide smile on her face. Her dark hair formed a warm waterfall rushing past her shoulders. Silver hoop earrings dangled from dainty ears to compliment the peach blush of her smooth cheeks. A short, black dress with a rhinestone belt emphasized her small waist, and was paired with white pumps.

Edison gulped at the sight and failed to notice Bree's parents standing behind her until she introduced them.

"Edison, this is my mother and father, Maricela and Enrique Mata." Bree's parents wore friendly smiles.

"Pleased to meet you," Edison managed to say.

Enrique, a slight man with thick, black hair leaned forward and shook Edison's hand. He chuckled and said, "Bree talks about you all the time. I'm glad we finally get to meet."

"Thank you, sir," Edison replied. He pulled at the collar of his shirt which suddenly felt too tight.

Bree saved him from further awkwardness by waving at her parents and shutting the door. They were halfway to the car before Edison remembered the corsage. He stopped and held it up. "This is for you."

Bree's hand went to her mouth. "Oh, it's so beautiful." She took it out of the plastic box and slipped the elastic band of the corsage over her wrist.

She dug her phone from the small purse and took a picture of the corsage. Then she held the cell at arm's length, leaned closer to Edison, and said, "Smile." Bree turned the phone and showed the picture to Edison. Two faces with bright smiles looked back at him.

As they continued on to the car, a warm feeling filled Edison. Carney was right.

Girls do like flowers.

Carney dropped Bree and Edison off at the school cafeteria.

Gaily covered ribbons and bunting framed the doors, and when they entered, dozens of balloons in the school's colors of red, white, and black, greeted them. A large handprinted banner hung from the ceiling: *Harpersville Junior High—District Football Champions.*

Already, over a hundred students packed the cafeteria and stood in groups as music blared. The hired DJ stood in a corner surrounded by an elaborate sound system. Arranged in a semicircle, the Bose speakers had laser lights mounted on stands beside them. Strobe-like, they flashed and blazed, the dancing teenagers illuminated in a stop-motion effect.

Bree led Edison to a corner where Hondo and Carly chatted among a throng of students.

Hondo wore a blue polo shirt and jeans. He held a slice of pizza in one hand and soft drink in the other. "Hey, Edison," he mumbled through a mouthful of the pizza. "Hey, Bree."

Next to him, Carly stood in a short, white skirt, and a form-fitting white blouse. Her hair, piled high on her head, still managed to look artful despite the casual arrangement.

Edison swallowed at the sight. *She's so pretty.*

A new tune cranked out and Hondo wolfed down the last of the pizza. He grabbed Carly's hand. "Let's go!" They raced to join the other students gyrating to the music.

Soon, Bree and Edison were by themselves. "Want to check out what kind of snacks they have?" Bree asked.

Before Edison could answer, a familiar—and unwelcome—figure ambled over.

"Jones! Didn't expect to see you here," Markie snickered. "You know this is called a *dance*, right?" He pointed at the anti-grav chair. "Unless that thing can grow legs, all you'll do is watch, just like all the other loser wallflowers."

He leaned closer. "What's it like, Jones? Watching and knowing you will never be able to hit the floor like everyone else? Do you get off on it?"

Moving to interpose herself between Edison and Markie, Bree's eyes flashed. "You are a horrible, mean *bastard!*"

A harsh laugh erupted from Markie. "Whoa. Bad language from the Queen of Clean? What's the world comin' to? Tell you what, even though you're still too skinny for me, if you get tired of watching and actually want to dance, just give me a wave." With another snort, he sauntered off.

Fists clenched, Bree took a step to follow the bully's retreating back. Edison caught her arm and shook his head. "Don't."

She stomped her foot. "I'm going to find one of the chaperons and get him thrown out!"

For the first time, Edison noticed Bree wasn't wearing her glasses. Even in the dim light, and her face flushed with anger, her brown eyes appeared soft and warm.

"You have..." He struggled to find the words, "I mean you don't have your glasses on," he stammered.

Distracted by the comment, Bree smiled, her braces on full display. "You noticed. I decided to wear contacts. What do you think?"

"They—they're beautiful. Your eyes I mean." His cheeks grew warm as the bold statement. *Did I just say that? What an idiot!*

Bree looked at him for a moment, then leaned over and kissed his cheek. "That's the nicest thing you have ever said to me." She stood, hesitated, then held out her hand.

Edison gulped, his entire body now having joined his cheeks in growing warm. Slowly, he lifted his arm and took her hand in his.

Side-by-side, Markie forgotten, Edison held Bree's hand while their friends and classmates danced and whirled.

"C'mon," Bree whispered in his ear. "We can dance too."

She led him to floor where they joined the other teenagers. Her grip never left his as he moved the anti-grav chair in unison with her.

What could have been a disaster, thanks to the Markie, turned into something completely unexpected.

The best night of Edison's life.

CHAPTER 37

Edison looked out the car window as the airplane hangar drew near.

Corrugated steel formed a cocoon arching high over the empty facility. The hanger doors were open, and Edison spotted a large plexiglass cage inside. A number of Breakstone employees stood beside the structure and turned at the sound of the approaching vehicle.

Stanton Jones swiveled in the front seat and looked back at Edison. "I'm still not convinced this is a good idea. Are you sure you want to go through with it?"

Edison nodded. "Yes, Grandpa."

"Well, I think this is nuts," chimed Carney. "Breakstone Industries is a cutthroat company. They'll do anything to beat their competition and make a buck."

"You got that right," said Hondo seated next to Edison. Hondo nudged him with his knee. "I tried talkin' sense to him, tried to tell him he couldn't trust the zombie twins, but he wouldn't listen."

Hondo was the only member of robotics team to accompany Edison. A dance competition kept Carly away, and a family trip caused Bree to miss.

Carney appealed to Jones. "Sir, I can turn around right now. Just give the word."

The LogicTech CEO shook his head. "The anti-gravity elevator is Edison's invention, and it's his call. Besides, the entire project is stuck in regulatory limbo, going nowhere."

Jones winked at Edison. "Although I put nothing past the Breakstones, I *do* trust my grandson. If he says he can win, then I believe him."

A warmth blossomed inside Edison. His fear Grandpa would prevent the 'bot competition never materialized. When he finally approached Stanton Jones to reveal his plans, his grandfather asked a number of questions before agreeing to let Edison participate. His only requirement was he and Carney accompany the team, along with a LogicTech security crew. Another SUV followed them filled with the security personnel.

Both SUVs pulled up to the hangar entrance. Grim-faced men spilled out of the trailing vehicle and flanked the Suburban. After Edison and the rest emerged, their armed escort accompanied them step-by-step to the battle cage.

A thin man in a dark suit approached them. Silver-blonde hair was immaculately swept back from his high forehead, while pale-blue eyes perched above a sharp nose studied them.

His lips pursed to form a narrow line at the sight of the security team. "Really, Stanton. Is this necessary?"

"Yes, Manfred, I think it is. Would you like me to elaborate on the reasons why?"

Manfred Breakstone chuckled, a sound which reminded Edison of the rasp of a rattlesnake's tail. "I see you continue to traffic in rumor and innuendo. How droll," he sneered.

Anger flashed across Jones' face. "When it comes to my family, I consider nothing to be droll. Now, let's get this over with."

A cruel smile spread across Breakstone's face. "By all means, *lets*. This way." He motioned toward the battle cage.

Edison studied the set-up, noting that the thick plexiglass

walls rose almost halfway to the hangar's curved ceiling. The glass encased an area roughly the size of a boxing ring. Portable stands were erected on either side of the battle cage. A stainless steel ball hung suspended above the enclosure. Blunt spikes, like shortened porcupine quills, covered its surface. At the sight, Edison's eyes narrowed.

"Manfred?" Hondo whispered. "The dude's name is Manfred? Where did the Breakstones get all these goofy names? If I had a name like that, I'd get my ass kicked every day."

Edison ignored his friend and continued to study the sphere perched above the cage. He pointed and said, "That looks like a laser array." He turned to Hondo. "The first evidence of cheating, although I'm certain it won't be the last."

As they walked further, Hillary and Heller emerged from the pack of Breakstone employees and stood side-by-side. Each wore a dark suit the exact duplicate of their father's, except Hillary who wore a skirt rather than slacks.

"Edison Jones," they greeted in unison.

"Are you prepared for defeat?" Hillary jeered.

"Yes, remember the terms of our agreement," Heller snickered. "When you lose, you will cease and desist from developing your space elevator."

Edison shrugged. "Just make sure you keep your end of the bargain when you lose."

The twins shared a look and laughed. "Shall we begin?" Heller asked. At Edison's nod, he motioned, and a 'bot emerged from a dark corner of the cavernous hanger and moved toward the open gate in the battle ring.

Oval-shaped, a black exoskeleton covered the robot. It gleamed in the light, and the shape reminded Edison of a giant ladybug. A dozen baseball-sized steel wheels were embedded beneath its structure. One look told Edison the 'bot had a three-hundred and sixty degree range of motion, and could, in an instant, stop and move in any direction.

"Julius Caesar once said, *I came; I saw; I conquered,*" Hillary remarked. She smirked at Edison. "We call our robot, *Caesar,* as undoubtedly, he will obliterate your battle robot." The twins pivoted and walked, lockstep, to the stands opposite LogicTech's.

Hondo's mouth dropped at the sight of Breakstone battle 'bot. "What's that black stuff covering their robot?"

"Carbon fiber…the toughest material on the planet," Edison replied tersely.

Team Edison's robot trundled out of an enclosed trailer the security team had backed up to the hangar. It resembled a Rubik's Cube with dozens of gray blocks molded into a single frame. The 'bot moved on a triple set of treads which swiveled to change direction.

Compared to the twin's sleek robot, Edison's automaton looked clumsy and slow. Laughter broke out from the Breakstone spectators at the sight of the robot missing the entry gate and slamming into the plexiglass. The 'bot backed up, turned, and finally managed to enter the battle cage.

Both robots positioned themselves to face each other on opposite sides of the cage.

Then waited for the signal to begin.

CHAPTER 38

A LARGE DIGITAL SCREEN COUNTED DOWN. AT ZERO, A SHRILL *BREEEP* filled the air.

The contest began.

The black robot shot forward. A slot opened in the armor, and a spinning saw emerged. Studded with industrial diamonds, an articulated metal arm extended the whirling blade forward.

Before Team Edison's 'bot could react, the saw began to cut into it. Sparks flew, and the robot backed away, but not before a long ragged slash decorated its flank. The treads pivoted and the 'bot sped away with surprising speed. The Breakstone battle robot followed, the *whir* of the blade reverberating off the glass enclosure.

Suddenly, Team Edison's 'bot, stopped, reversed direction, and slammed into the pursuing automaton. The clash of metal against metal, sent the smaller black, battle robot spinning out of control. It crashed into the wall and remained motionless.

Hondo cheered. "Take that!"

Before he could make another comment, the Breakstone 'bot righted itself, and raced toward Team Edison's robot. Another opening appeared in the exoskeleton to reveal an appendage with a blunt, anvil-like head. Attached to a piston, the gleaming steel thrust forward like a jousting lance. The LogicTech bot's treads pivoted and fled from its pursuing adversary.

Both 'bots sped round-and-round the ring. Breakstone's automaton slowly closed the distance, and suddenly, with a *whoosh*, the lance catapulted from the piston. The heavy bolt struck Team Edison's robot with such impact, that it lifted the automaton temporarily off its treads. A softball-sized dent appeared on its flank, and seconds later, the *whir* of the cutting saw commenced again. The *shriek* of metal cutting metal echoed as the larger, slower 'bot tried to extricate itself. Finally, the LogicTech automaton tore away, another laceration marring its structure.

Carney grimaced and looked at Edison. "Why doesn't your robot defend itself? Why doesn't it fight back?"

Edison smiled. "Just waiting for the right time."

With a *crash*, Team Edison's 'bot reversed direction and again, rammed its opponent. This time, the Breakstone robot quickly recovered and sped after the LogicTech automaton.

Without warning, a *hum* vibrated off the walls of the cage, and pencil-thin beams of intense light erupted from the globe suspended above the battle ring. The red shafts formed a network which cross-crossed the floor. Unable to stop in time, Team Edison's robot ran right through one of the beams. The smell of melting, scorched metal wafted in the air.

A section of the LogicTech 'bot sheared off.

Attempting to escape the searing lasers, the 'bot blundered through several more beams, pieces falling off like pats of butter before coming to a shuddering stop near the wall of the enclosure. The Breakstone automaton easily avoided the laser array, and moved in for the kill.

"The twins programmed the pattern of the laser array into their robot before the contest," Edison observed. "That's how their 'bot avoids the lasers. Naturally, they didn't tell us."

Hondo shook his head. "I know you talked about this variable thing, but it doesn't look good."

Edison grinned at his friend. "It's not supposed to look good, remember? That's part of the plan. Just wait a bit longer."

Hondo shook his head. "I know, but it's hard to watch."

The boys returned their attention to the battle arena.

The Breakstone robot pummeled Team Edison's battle 'bot. Pounding away with the ram-like piston and cutting deeply with the diamond saw, the LogicTech 'bot shuddered and tried to escape, but parts of the automaton lay smoking and scattered all over the floor. It managed to travel a few feet before it stopped, toppled over…and lay still.

A roar rose from the Breakstone side. Hillary and Heller wore smug looks as they stood and approached Edison. They stopped beside his anti-grav chair.

"We win," Hillary said.

"Yes, the outcome was never in doubt," Heller added.

Edison crossed his arms. "The contest isn't over."

Heller laughed. "Of course it is. Your robot is disabled."

Hillary pointed. "Look, it lies in pieces—"

The words died in her mouth.

Team Edison's robot began to dissolve. A steady stream of ant-sized specks scurried from the blocks forming the robot's cubic shape. Each individual cube disgorged the miniature particles at a dizzying pace and appeared to be melting away.

Hondo grinned at the expression on the twins' faces. "Hey, Wednesday and Pugsley? You two look a little confused. Ever hear of Nanobots? Didn't know anything about nanotechnology myself until Edison explained it to me. It's all still a little fuzzy in my head, but I *did* understand taking big things and making them smaller. Do you need me to describe nanotechnology—"

"We know what it means!" Hillary snarled.

Hondo's grin grew even wider. "Good. Then let's sit back and watch the show."

The first line of nanobots reached the Breakstone robot and began to climb up its flanks. The black automaton tried to run them over, but for every nanobot crushed beneath the steel wheels, a dozen scampered up its side. Neither did the club-like piston or the diamond saw help slow the parade. The miniscule 'bots were simply too small. In fact, the open slots in the robot's exoskeleton provided entry points for the tiny 'bots, and they poured inside.

A short time later, smoke rose from inside the battle robot, followed by the acrid smell of burnt wiring. The Breakstone 'bot started to act erratically, and blundered into the maze of the laser array. Whole sections sheared away, the metal bubbling and sizzling. Moments later, the battle 'bot lay inert and in numerous pieces.

The nanobots exited the remains and formed columns which scurried for the gate exiting the battle cage. Once outside, they began to stack and join into larger and larger units. Moments later, the original, cubic-shaped robot formed once again.

Edison looked at the astonished faces of Hillary and Heller. "Game over. You lose."

He reached up and high-fived Hondo. "And Team Edison wins!"

Hillary's face twisted. "You broke the rules. You can have only one robot, not hundreds."

"Not thousands," Heller added.

Edison crossed his arms. "The CRIO directly controls the 'bots. The rules state there is no limit to the CRIO memory and data capacity. My CRIO controls all the nanobots, and therefore *is* the battle 'bot."

The twins looked ready to argue the point when Manfred Breakstone strolled up. He motioned with his head, and Hillary and Heller spun and stalked away.

He glared at Edison. "Congratulations. You win this round."

A thin smile appeared on his face. "We'll see how long your winning streak lasts."

He pivoted and disappeared into the throng of Breakstone employees.

CHAPTER 39

"Look at this!" Edison shoved a letter into Hondo's hand.

The two boys were waiting in the parent pick-up area adjacent to Harpersville Junior High. The last day of school before the week-long Thanksgiving break, cars were lined up three deep down the entire asphalt road.

Puzzled, Hondo took the letter and studied it. "Hey, this is from NASA."

"We've got the green light from NASA to conduct another test of the space elevator."

"You're kidding!" Hondo exclaimed. "You mean the Breakstones actually came through? I never would have believed it in a million years."

Edison shook his head. "I know. It's hard for me to believe too." He turned to his friend and crowed, "But it doesn't matter, because *now* we can move forward! We've scheduled a test for next weekend."

Barely able to control his enthusiasm, Edison gushed, "We already have a new launch vehicle ready to take the place of the prototype. We've upgraded the anti-gravity coils, used the data from the first test to refine the parabolic drift, and fixed the problems with the stabilization gyros."

Hondo stared at Edison. "Uh, that's great...I think."

Edison laughed. "It means we worked all the bugs out. This space elevator is bigger, more powerful, and faster."

Hondo brightened. "Well, why didn't you say that in the first place?"

A big SUV with a LogicTech logo pulled into the line a dozen car lengths away. The vehicle inched along as the automobiles in front pulled up, and parents picked up their children. Edison pointed. "There's our ride."

Fidgeting as the SUV drew closer, Hondo finally blurted, "Hey, can I stay with you next week?"

Puzzled, Edison turned, "But you're already spending the weekend at the mansion."

"Yeah, I know, but my mom's new boyfriend moved in. I don't get along with him any better than the others." Hondo shoved his hands in his pockets and stared at the ground.

Edison's excitement over the new test launch evaporated. *Can't Hondo's mother see what's going on? Why does she let these boyfriends abuse him?*

He searched for words, finally saying, "I'll ask Grandpa when we get home. I'm sure it will be okay."

The relief on Hondo's face was palpable. Carney rolled to a stop, and the boys got into the SUV.

The burly bodyguard pulled out, and they headed for the Jones Mansion.

Once home, Edison approached Stanton Jones about Hondo spending the entire week with them. "Hondo never wants to stay at home, Grandpa. He doesn't like these guys that stay with his mother. I'm pretty sure he gets beat up by them sometimes."

His grandfather's nostrils flared. "I see. Has he ever reported these incidents?"

Edison shook his head. "No, and please don't tell him I said anything to you, Grandpa! He doesn't like to talk about it much."

Jones nodded. He sighed and leaned toward Edison. "Of course. However, you understand there may come a point when you have to tell someone in authority?"

Edison nodded, his emotions wrestling back and forth. *One day Hondo might get hurt really bad, and it might be my fault because I didn't say anything. But if I talk to the counselor at school or anyone else, he'll just get mad at me. He won't understand.*

His hands twisted in his lap. "It's not always easy to know the right thing to do, is it, Grandpa?"

Jones squeezed Edison's shoulder. "No. No it's not." He straightened, and smiled. "But I'm confident if you are ever forced to make a choice, you'll make the right one. Why don't you go find Hondo, and we'll have him call his mother."

Relieved, Edison whizzed away on his hoverchair and returned a short time later with Hondo. His big friend flipped out his phone, and a terse conversation ensued. It ended when he handed his cell to Edison's grandfather. Stanton Jones listened then nodded.

"Very good, Mrs. Edwards. We'll take good care of your son."

He handed the phone back to Hondo and winked. "Looks like you're staying with us for Thanksgiving."

The boys hooted and headed for Edison's room. Once there, they took the pneumatic car to the underground lab where the young scientist tested the algorithms to be used in the launch of the space elevator.

Hondo grabbed a controller and directed the robotic forklift around the cavernous structure. The machine picked up pallets, boxes, and other various objects, then retracted the treads. With a *whoosh*, the forklift floated on a cushion of air, and Hondo spun it round and round like a top.

"Who needs PlayStation when you got one of these?" he gushed.

Edison paused and looked up. "What's a PlayStation?"

Hondo's mouth worked, but no sound came out. Astonished, he managed to ask, "You don't know what a PlayStation is?"

Edison shook his head.

Hondo powered down the forklift and placed the controller on a lab table. "You invented an anti-gravity elevator, but don't know what the most popular video gaming device on the planet is?" He shook his head. "Man, you must have never got out—"

He clamped his mouth shut. Face red, Hondo pulled a chair over and sat by Edison. "Sorry. My mouth kinda runs past my mind sometimes. I know what you've been through."

Edison waved his hand. "It's okay." He shut down the computer. "And you're right. I didn't get out much."

He folded his hands in his lap. "There's a lot I need to catch up on. The stuff I invent—the science and technology—comes easy to me."

Edison thought of the challenges Hondo faced every day at home. "But what's hard is understanding people, especially kids my age. I don't always get it, and it can be so frustrating..." His voice trailed off.

Hondo shrugged. "Nah. I think you *get* a lot more than you think. Anyway, what do I know? My own family put the capital 'M' in messed up. I got no room to talk."

Hondo laughed and shook his head. "What a pair we are, huh, Edison?"

Grinning, Edison said, "I guess so." He pointed upward. "Want to go swimming? The indoor pool is heated."

"Are you kidding? Race you to the elevator!"

Whooping, the boys made their way to the lift.

Hours later, exhausted from swimming, Edison lay in bed on the edge of sleep. Drowsy thoughts drifted through his mind. One in particular brought a smile to his lips. *You get a lot more than you think*, Hondo said. *And if it is good enough for Hondo…*

It's good enough for me.

CHAPTER 40

The week of Thanksgiving ushered in frenetic activity as preparations were made for the next test of the space elevator.

Technicians swarmed over the launch module and anti-gravity coils. The launch program and protocols were refined through repeated dry runs until Edison was satisfied no technical glitches remained. Because he knew just how busy he would be, Edison gave Hondo a security card and use of one of the LogicTech's battery-powered carts. Given the run of the huge underground facility, his friend wasted no time exploring.

Hondo soon became a familiar figure at the fabrication, research, and other workstations. He passed through security checkpoints so frequently, he knew the guards on a first name basis, and they just waved him through. One of the security personnel had a son that played on the football team with Hondo, and he tossed a football with Hondo every time he passed his guard station.

All work stopped on Thanksgiving as the LogicTech employees spent the holiday with their families, then picked up again in earnest on Friday, the following day. With time on his hands, Edison continued to run computer simulations of the anti-grav elevator searching for any problem, no matter how small, which might derail a successful launch.

The hours flew by, and morning passed into afternoon. Finally, Edison sat back and released a satisfied sigh.

Perfect. Everything is perfect.

He manipulated the controls, and his anti-grav chair took him to the lift. He found Hondo in the kitchen eating leftover turkey and dressing. Edison grinned at his friend's bottomless appetite.

"You want to go swimming again? We have a few hours before dinner."

"Thought you'd never ask!" Hondo shoved a few more mouthfuls of dressing into his mouth and charged for the pool.

By the time Edison caught up, Hondo had already changed into his trunks and dove into the water. When Carney came to retrieve them for supper, both boys were pleasantly tired and ravenous. Edison had second helpings of the roast beef, mashed potatoes and gravy, although Hondo far surpassed him. His large friend helped himself to thirds and fourths.

Later that night, Edison found he had no trouble sleeping. Although keyed up over the next day's launch, the combination of swimming and a big meal left him drowsy even as he slid into bed. Within moments, he fell fast asleep.

A persistent shaking pulsed through Hondo's shoulder. "Time to get up!" a voice cried.

Hondo rolled over on his back and through bleary eyes, spied Edison.

"What time is it?"

"Almost nine o'clock. Carly and Bree will be here in an hour."

Hondo turned back onto his stomach and pulled the blanket over his head. "Then I got plenty of time," he said.

"Not if you want to eat breakfast."

The sheets flew off and Hondo rolled to his feet.

Edison laughed. "Thought that would get your attention."

"Even Superman has his kryptonite. Mine is food," Hondo grumbled as he stumbled into the bathroom.

He was still wolfing down scrambled eggs and sausage when Carly and Bree arrived. Carly plopped down next to him. Chin cupped in her hand, she said, "So you stayed all week with Edison?"

"Yep." He wiped his mouth with a napkin, and with a sigh, sat back.

"I bet you two had a lot of fun."

Hondo shrugged. "Well, I didn't see Edison much during the day. He's been busy with his space elevator stuff. I spent most of the time tooling around the underground LogicTech labs. You should see the place. It's so big they have tunnels with roads and even stoplights—"

He snapped his fingers and sat up. "Hey, you want to see it? The launch isn't until this afternoon." He dug his security pass out of his pocket. "Edison gave me a cart, and I can go anywhere I want."

Carly jumped up. "Let's go."

Hondo stood, eager to get started. "I'll tell Edison—"

He paused. Edison and Bree were nowhere to be seen. "Hey, where did they go?"

Carly giggled. "I saw them headed for the indoor pool and garden." She leaned closer. "Bree likes Edison and I think he likes her too."

Hondo worked his jaw as if tasting a new flavor. "Wait. Edison likes a girl?"

Carly crossed her arms. "Yes. I understand this happens quite a bit."

"But, why?"

Carly stepped back and frowned. "Why? You mean because Edison has a disability he can't like girls?"

Hondo felt his face flush. "No", he stammered. "Edison can like anyone he wants."

For a moment Carly stood tapping her foot. Finally, she said, "Well, I'm glad he has your approval." A smile returned to her face. "Hondo?"

"Yeah?"

"I wonder who *you* like?"

The heat in Hondo's face jumped to an egg frying temperature. Rather than answer, he turned and hurried to the downstairs lift adjacent to the hallway. The private elevator, although not as much fun as Edison's pneumatic one, went directly to the LogicTech facility. As he waited for Carly, a thought occurred to him.

Edison's not the only one who doesn't always get it.

CHAPTER 41

"Shouldn't we wait for Hondo and Carly?" Edison swiveled his anti-grav chair and looked behind him.

Bree reached out and grabbed the hoverchair. It bobbed up and down in her grasp, but she turned it around easily. "Don't worry about them. I want to see the indoor garden. I love the flowers and palm trees."

"But don't you think—"

Bree gave the anti-gravity chair a hard shove, and it floated backward several feet. Hands on hips, she asked, "Why can't we go by ourselves?"

Edison blinked. Bree crossed her arms, a firm look on her face. Impatient, she tossed her head, long dark hair rippling in the light. "Well?"

"Uh, okay."

"Good. Let's go." After a moment's hesitation, Edison had the anti-grav chair moving again. Bree took the lead, and he followed closely behind.

A short time later, they came to the atrium. The scent of tropical flowers drifted in the air, the babble of water from the artificial stream a soft whisper. They followed the winding, flagstone path until they came to a marble bench. Bree stopped and sat down.

She motioned for Edison to join her.

He glided up to her, and was about to speak when Bree leaned forward and placed a kiss on his lips.

A hundred different emotions thundered through Edison, each demanding to be heard. Numbness, surprise, and elation followed in rapid succession. His heart pounded and threatened to leap from his chest.

Bree stood and turned to Edison.

"*Now* we can go look for Hondo and Carly."

The wheels on the LogicTech cart hummed as Hondo negotiated the broad, underground corridors. Having already taken Carly to several of the research centers, he laughed while she looked around in wide-eyed wonder.

Much to his relief, she didn't bring up who he liked again.

"Where are we going now?" Carly asked.

Hondo grinned. "I saved the best for last. You'll see."

An intersection appeared, and he turned right and accelerated. The roadway soon ended in front of two colossal doors. They extended to the ceiling, over a hundred feet in height and twice that in width.

Hondo stopped and hopped off the cart. He trotted to a control panel and looked back at Carly. "Watch this."

He flashed his security pass over a recessed scanner. A deep rumble echoed off the walls, and the massive doors began to slide apart. Sensors detected their presence, and banks of lights clicked on as they entered.

The spacious warehouse held only one object; a barrel-shaped module. In an upright position, four rigid cylindrical arms extended from the structure, each ending in a pancake-shaped ring. An observation port of thick, tinted glass occupied a space about halfway up the module's gleaming metal flank. Below and to the side of the port, the faint outline of an oval hatch appeared. Like sprigs of grass, an array of communication devices sprouted from different locations on the metallic exterior.

Carly stared in amazement. "What is it?"

"That's *Journey II*, the launch vehicle Edison's going to send into space."

The hatch popped open suddenly, and a LogicTech guard stuck his head out and blinked in the light. His dark eyes widened at the sight of Hondo and Carly.

"Hey, what are you doing here?"

A voice came from within the open hatch, demanding, "Who the devil are you talking to?"

"There's a couple of kids out here," the guard replied.

"What? Get out of my way!"

The guard jumped out and headed for Hondo and Carly. A short time later, another man exited the module. Dressed in an expensive blue suit, he straightened his tie and followed the security guard. He stopped in front of the young pair, and scowled.

"Who are you? Why are you here?"

Hondo stared at the man. Then recognition flickered in his mind. "Wait a second. You're the guy from NASA. The dude who thought Edison's space elevator wouldn't work."

Hondo's eyes narrowed. "What are you doing here? The launch isn't until this afternoon."

An evil chuckle bubbled from Cutter Gentry. "Oh, that's simple enough to answer. We're going to make sure this next test of the anti-gravity elevator fails."

The NASA official shook his head. "What a shame. Just a few more minutes and our work here would have been finished."

He leaned forward. "But instead, you've seen us and interrupted our sabotage."

A nasty smirk split Gentry's face. "'Timing is everything' they say, and unfortunately, yours is abysmal."

He slipped his hand inside his suit jacket and took out a slim, tapered pistol. He pointed it at the young pair then pulled the trigger.

Pfft, Pfft. A tiny blue dart sprouted from Hondo's chest. An identical barb protruded from Carly. She took a breath to scream, but instead, released a soft moan before her eyes rolled back in her head and she collapsed.

Hondo shook his head to clear a fog that became thicker and thicker. His legs, boneless and rubbery, refused to cooperate.

Moments later, he joined Carly on the floor.

The guard knelt by the pair. He growled, "Out cold. What do you want me to do with them?"

Gentry tapped his lips. "Disable and get rid of their cell phones. Then make sure you've wiped the security footage for the past two hours. I'll take care of these two."

His smirk widened. "I've got the perfect solution on how to eliminate them as a problem."

CHAPTER 42

EDISON'S THOUGHTS WERE A HAPPY, JUMBLED MESS.

Several times he touched his lips and replayed the memory of Bree's kiss. The upcoming test of his space elevator seemed light years away instead of only hours. Before Bree's one brief kiss, he was laser-focused on the launch. Now he was completely sidetracked.

"Edison."

He blinked. They were back at the mansion and in the spacious den, the time after the kiss a complete blur.

"*Edison!*"

He looked up at Bree's worried face.

"Carly won't answer my calls. Her phone goes straight to voice mail. I've texted her over and over, and she doesn't reply."

Edison scratched his head. "Maybe she's busy."

Bree threw up her hands. "You don't understand. Carly always has her phone. She would have called or texted me back by now."

She pulled a chair next to Edison. "Besides, we had a plan. We were each going to go off by ourselves, me with you, and Carly with Hondo."

She twisted her hands in her lap. "I wanted to be alone with you, and she wanted to be alone with Hondo."

Stunned, Edison sat back.

"Don't you see? Carly would have her phone and definitely would have called or texted me by now. She wouldn't be able to wait to know what happened between us."

Edison tried to make sense of what Bree was saying. "You mean this is all part of some scheme? A game? Something you and Carly…" his voice trailed off.

The happy memory of Bree's warm lips dissolved. The hurt on his face must have been obvious, because Bree shot up and knelt by his side. She took his hand in hers.

"I like you Edison. But I know you're shy, and I just wanted to speed things up a bit."

Her comment took some of the sting out of her confession about *the plan*. He cleared his throat. "If they're in the underground facility, cell phones won't work down there."

Bree shook her head. "I thought of that, but Hondo already gave us the password and how to connect with the LogicTech Wi-Fi and communication system. The first thing Carly would have done is sync her phone to the system."

Bree stood. "Something is definitely wrong. Carly would never go anywhere without her cell. Its attached to her like a third arm or leg."

Edison had never seen Bree so worried. "Let me try. *Call Hondo*," he said. His cell lit up, but after one ring, it went straight to voice mail.

Puzzled, Edison sat back. *There must be a logical explanation.* But try as he might, nothing came to mind.

Deep in thought, his phone beeped loudly. Startled, he almost dropped it. Eagerly, he swiped it, but instead of Hondo, he saw the face of his grandpa.

Stanton Jones smiled. "Are you ready for your big day? I'm at the control center. We need to go over a few details prior to the activation of the anti-gravity elevator, so go ahead and make your way over here."

"Sure, Grandpa," Edison replied.

He looked up at Bree, concern still etched on her features. "I've got to get to the launch center. Once I'm there, I'll talk to Grandpa and see if he can have Carney look for Hondo and Bree." He flashed a smile. "I'm sure everything will be okay."

They made their way to the mansion's garage where Edison transferred into a four-seater cart. His anti-grav chair hovered to the back, folded up, and dropped into the vehicle's cargo hatch. With a *whisk*, one of the bay doors slid upward, sunlight streaming into the six car garage.

Edison glanced at Bree. "Be sure you're buckled up securely."

Puzzled, she asked, "Why?"

Edison grinned. "Because I've supercharged the power cells on this cart." He pushed the throttle forward, and they shot out onto the circular drive. Tires screeching, they exited onto an asphalt road leading to the control center.

Trees, ponds, and grassy fields rushed by, Bree's hair billowing behind her. The ribbon of blacktop curved around a grove of oak, and the control center came into view. The tower stretched skyward, over four stories tall. Tinted glass completely encircled the topmost section, the dark glass glinting in the late morning light. Three circular concrete aprons lay perpendicular to the control center. The first and smallest was the size of a helicopter landing pad, the next the size of a medium-sized parking lot, while the last pad could easily contain a football field.

A number of LogicTech vehicles were parked at the base of the tower. As Edison pulled up and parked the cart, he spotted a sedan with the NASA logo stenciled on the side. Curious, he slid out of the seat and onto his hover chair. Bree joined him moments later, a flush on her cheeks from the wind and exhilarating ride. Edison fought to keep a smile off his face.

At least I got her mind off Carly.

In the control center, they were met by a pair of uniformed LogicTech guards. Waved through, they took the elevator to the top observation level. There, technicians scurried about in a hum of activity. Banks of computers, communications, and other equipment were powered up and tested.

Edison looked around and spotted his grandfather standing next to a vaguely familiar figure. When he reached Stanton Jones, the man turned revealing a lanyard containing a NASA badge and ID.

Cutter Gentry.

The NASA official raised an eyebrow. "Well, if it isn't the boy genius himself. Let's hope this second test of your anti-gravity elevator goes more smoothly than the first."

Gentry rocked back on his heels. "If not," he waved his hand, "then I'll be forced to recommend it a failure and end NASA's interest in your project." With a smirk, he turned and walked away.

Edison's dislike for the man deepened. *It's like he wants a botched test.*

He felt a tug on his arm and looked to see Bree motion with her chin at his grandfather. "Oh!" He'd completely forgotten about Carly.

Edison cleared his throat. "Grandpa, can you get someone to find Hondo and Carly? We think they're in the underground annex, but we can't get them to answer a text or a call even though they know how to sync to the LogicTech communication system."

Stanton Jones frowned. "*Hmm.* That's strange." He fished his cell from his pocket and pressed a button. After a short conversation, he turned back to Edison and Bree.

"Carney's got a team looking for them." He winked at Bree. "I wouldn't worry about your friends. The facility is enormous, and they are probably just curious and still looking around."

Relieved, Edison sat back. He was confident the ex-SEAL would find them soon. Besides, Hondo spent the entire week exploring the underground facility, and by now, should know every nook and cranny.

What could possibly go wrong?

CHAPTER 43

As the two o'clock time for the test of the space elevator drew nearer, Edison found himself immersed in last minute details and the precheck launch list. So intent on his task, he didn't notice Carney exit the elevator until a hand tapped his shoulder. Startled, Edison turned and looked up.

The ex-SEAL, his grandfather beside him, wore a grim look on his face. "We can't find your friends anywhere in the underground annex."

"Could they have gone back up to the mansion?" Jones asked,

Carney shook his head. "We already checked. We searched every nook and cranny from top to bottom. And, before you ask, we did the same for the labs and research facilities. We even sent a robot-cam through the ductwork. Nothing."

A sense of foreboding crept up Edison's spine. "What about the security cameras? They should have been able to track everywhere they went."

Carney's lips flattened into a thin line. "The entire system went offline two hours ago. One of our IT guys managed to restart it, and that's when we discovered the morning's footage had been erased."

Bree joined them and overheard the exchange. "Erased? You mean like somebody did it on purpose?"

Carney hesitated. "We don't know that for sure—yet. We're still checking." He turned and made eye contact with Stanton Jones. "There are too many coincidences here, sir. I suggest a full lockdown of the facilities until we've found these kids. In the meantime, I can organize another search team and sweep the entire area and facilities again."

The LogicTech CEO nodded. "Under the circumstances, I don't see other options. We'll just reschedule the test—"

"*What!*"

The shout came from across the room.

Cutter Gentry stormed toward the group. "Did I hear you correctly? Reschedule the test of your anti-gravity elevator?"

Stanton Jones frowned. "Edison's friends are lost somewhere in the underground annex. Their safety comes first, and we have to find them."

Gentry waved his arms. "What are you running here, Jones? A daycare center or an aerospace research facility?" Red-faced, he stabbed his finger at Edison. "I tried to talk my superiors out of this fool's errand after your last fiasco but was overruled. The best minds in the business have been working on propulsion systems for decades, yet here I'm forced to spend my valuable time on something developed by a kid barely out of diapers."

He whirled on Jones. "If you cancel the test after all the time and trouble NASA went through to set up this observation, I can promise you there will not be another!"

Stanton Jones held Gentry's gaze with an icy stare. "That sounds like a threat. Let me remind you the expense of this test has been borne exclusively by LogicTech. NASA hasn't spent a dime on the development of the anti-gravity elevator. Perhaps a call to someone above your pay grade is in order."

Gentry chuckled, his smirk a twisted mask. "Go ahead. Call away. The NASA bureaucracy works at the same speed as the rest of the federal government—slow, slower, and glacial. By the time your complaint is received, processed, studied, and a decision made, it could be next year or even the year after."

Red crept up the CEO's neck, and his eyes flashed. Before he could provide a retort, Carney interjected, "Sir, the search wouldn't be affected at all by the space elevator test." He speared Gentry with a steely gaze. "And when we find Edison's friends, we can *all* celebrate the success of his anti-gravity elevator."

Jones looked at Edison. "What do you think? Postpone the launch or go ahead with it?"

Edison, still smarting from Gentry's comments, found his irritation with the man going from a simmer to a full boil. Concern for his friends washed away in a sea of red anger.

I'll show you!

Jaw set, he said, "I'm ready, Grandpa. All the pre-check protocols are in the green, and we're prepared for launch." He turned toward Gentry. "The elevator will set the space module in a stable orbit and then retrieve it. The entire process will be flawless. I guarantee it!"

Edison's hoverchair spun and shot back to the banks of instruments. He punched a button and digital numbers flashed on the monitors spaced around the observation tower.

The countdown had begun.

Edison watched as the module rode a motorized gurney to the mid-sized launch apron. With a *whir*, the gurney's platform lowered the spacecraft to the hard surface.

Once the concrete pad was vacated, Edison activated the onboard flight controls. As before, the anti-gravity elevator and the entire launch sequence would be controlled by computers. Having run the program countless times, Edison knew the mistakes associated with the first test had been corrected.

This test will be perfect.

Edison scrolled through the data on his screen and stopped at the sight of a trouble beacon blinking. He tapped the touchscreen, and the mass of the launch vehicle appeared. He leaned closer at the slight discrepancy in the module's total mass. At over twenty metric tons, or forty-five thousand pounds, the additional weight was slight, only about one hundred and twenty seven kilograms, or two hundred and eighty pounds. Precise mass—always an important factor in any space launch—had to be exact to calculate the thrust needed to overcome earth's gravity.

Under normal circumstances, a rocket was used to reach escape velocity—the minimum speed needed to escape earth's gravitational pull—and lift a payload into space. The heavier the payload, the more powerful the rocket needed to be. However, the anti-gravity elevator used a different principle. The push came, not from rocket thrusters, but from an artificial gravity field produced by rings containing powerful electromagnets. Once in a stable geosynchronous orbit, these same rings would then reverse their polarity and pull the space vehicle back to earth.

The tiny amount of added weight—like the addition of a flea to a dog's mass—was so insignificant, Edison pushed the anomaly aside.

All that mattered now was to make sure the space elevator worked perfectly, and make Cutter Gentry eat his words!

A soft but persistent chime broadcast into the control tower. *"Fifteen minutes to launch, fifteen minutes to launch,"* a pleasant female voice intoned.

Like a sprinter reacting to the report of a starter's pistol, Edison's mind soared into overdrive. He scrolled through every detail and all the preparations for the test of the anti-gravity elevator. He nodded, satisfied everything was in order. The minuscule discrepancy in the launch vehicle's mass posed no problem. Only—

Where did it come from? And how did it get there?

CHAPTER 44

A SHARP *CHIRP, CHIRP, CHIRP* ANNOUNCED THE LAUNCH SEQUENCE. The observation windows were crowded shoulder-to-shoulder, with personnel as they watched the barrel-shaped module gradually rise from the tarmac. Edison, eyes glued to the status readout on the monitor, heaved a sigh of relief.

All systems still in the green.

As it continued to rise, the spacecraft rotated slowly to reveal *Journey II* stenciled in black letters on the fuselage. At the sight, a cheer went up from the assembly of LogicTech engineers and technicians. A thrill coursed through Edison at the sound, and a wide smile grew across his face.

Like rhinestone bracelets, the anti-gravity rings glittered in the sunlight as they followed the space vehicle in an upward trajectory. As the ground fell away, the rings began to separate, the distance between them growing. The observers in the control tower craned their necks to follow the progress, the space module and anti-grav disks becoming smaller and smaller. Soon, *Journey II* became no more than a white speck—the only evidence of the anti-gravity rings an occasional metallic glint.

The passage through the layers of the atmosphere occurred with no issues except for some turbulence when the *Journey II* entered and exited the jet stream in the upper reaches of the troposphere. By this time, Edison had activated the onboard cameras, and the visuals of the rapidly shrinking earth were stunning. White clouds scudded across the surface, the oceans a deep azure blue. Rivers appeared like the coils of giant snakes meandering across the surface, while mountain ranges seemed like ridges and ripples molded from potter's clay.

Soon, a dark tint appeared. The atmosphere, thinner and thinner, began to lose color and give way to the dark vacuum of space. When *Journey II* passed through the thermosphere and entered the exosphere, the blackness became absolute. Minutes later, the ascent was complete.

Journey II reached stable orbital status.

"*Geosynchronous orbit, geosynchronous orbit,*" the computer's pleasant female voice intoned.

The announcement was met with an explosion of happy shouts, claps, and cheers. Edison shook his fists, and joined the tumultuous celebration with his own hoots of joy. He glanced at Cutter Gentry, and the NASA official—politely clapping with everyone else—but with a decided lack of enthusiasm. In fact, he looked like he had swallowed the world's largest lemon.

Edison checked the chronometer on the digital clock. Fourteen minutes and ten seconds.

The entire launch and placement in stable orbit took less than fifteen minutes!

The first test of *Journey I* took an arduous forty-five minutes, every second of it taunt and filled with tension. However, the module's descent and return morphed into the most hair-raising experience of Edison's life. It made this second launch feel like a cakewalk.

I never want to go through anything like that again.

Relief coursed through Edison at the prospect of a seamless return to earth of *Journey II*. A chuckle spilled from his lips, and he turned his attention to the streams of data scrolling across the monitor. Since all of it would be stored for later study, he skimmed over much of it until an oddity caught his eye.

Bob the Mannequin had been upgraded for this second test. Like before, he was designed to mimic the biological systems of the human body as closely as possible. Bob's data would then be used to measure the actual effect of the anti-gravity elevator on a living being. The data stream showed no abnormalities save one.

Instead of a single heartbeat from Bob, there were multiple heartbeats.

"What?" Edison mouthed.

He switched to the onboard cameras inside the module, and zoomed in on Bob. The mannequin, strapped tightly into the G-couch, sat upright and motionless. Nothing seemed out of place.

Puzzled, Edison studied the data again. "Isolate Bob's life metrics," he ordered the computer. The results appeared seconds later, and Edison's jaw dropped.

Besides the mannequin's artificial heart beat, two others appeared.

A dread premonition crawled over Edison's skin. "Locate the source of the other life signs," he sputtered.

After a short delay, the computer announced, "Storage bay, Section C."

Behind Bob's launch chair was a small cargo area recessed into the interior fuselage. Accessed by a metal panel, Edison directed the interior cameras to focus on the cargo bin. "Zoom in."

The next words tumbled from his mouth in a rush. "Open the storage bay." With a *hiss*, the door slid open.

Edison's blood froze at the sight the open compartment revealed.

Hondo and Carly floated unconscious side-by-side.

CHAPTER 45

TIME GROUND TO A HALT.

Edison stared, his mouth working soundlessly. Seconds later, the awful realization crashed down on him with the impact of an avalanche.

His friends were on the Journey II...in the vacuum of outer space!

"Grandpa," he tried to shout, but all that issued from his mouth was a whisper. Edison tried again. "Grandpa," he said, his voice rising to a hoarse croak. He took a deep breath. "GRANDPA!" he yelled.

Stanton Jones whipped his head around and hurried to Edison's side. "What's the—"

The words died in his throat at the sight Edison pointed to.

His grandfather's face mirrored Edison's own horror. "What? How?"

Edison's brain finally engaged. "I don't know how they got onboard, but we have to make sure the life support systems are functioning at their optimal level!"

Fortunately, part of *Journey II*'s assessment included a full test of the life support systems. Fear rode the edge of Edison's mind as he scanned the oxygen and temperature levels.

Normal.

A sigh of relief hissed from his lips. Quickly, he turned his attention to the readout of the radiation levels inside the module.

Also normal.

By this time, all the LogicTech employees crowded around the monitors displaying the unconscious pair. The noise level rose from a low babble to a chaotic rumble as dozens of voices competed to be heard.

Stanton Jones strode to the middle of the room. "Listen to me!" he thundered. His voice cut through the room like a laser. The chatter stopped immediately, all eyes focused on the LogicTech CEO.

"Obviously, we have a situation. From this moment on, all our efforts are to be dedicated to the safe return of *Journey II* and the kids onboard. Whatever your assigned task was before, drop it and prioritize only on the module's landing and maintaining peak efficiency of life support. Nothing else matters!"

After a moment's hesitation, the control tower exploded into action. Engineers, technicians, and support personnel rushed to comply. Dodging employees, Cutter Gentry weaved his way to where Stanton Jones stood and peered over Edison's shoulder at the monitor.

"I hate to say I told you so, but—"

Jones whirled to face the NASA official before he could finish. Nose-to-nose with Gentry, he hissed, "Then don't. In the meantime, unless you have something useful to contribute, stay the hell out of the way!"

Gentry smirked, then raised his hands and backed off. "Of course. Anything NASA can do to help, our full resources are at your disposal."

Edison heard the exchange but his mind had already leaped ahead. They needed to return *Journey II* back to earth immediately, and all his attention remained on that singular task.

Jones returned to Edison's side. "How are they doing?"

Edison shook his head. "Their life metrics appear okay except for a marked slowdown of metabolism and heartbeat. It's almost like—"

He turned to face his grandpa. "Like they have been drugged."

Jones' expression hardened. "That would explain their unconscious state. Unfortunately, it doesn't explain why they were drugged, or how they got aboard the module." He tapped the monitor. "How fast can we get them home? Once we have them safely back on the surface, then we'll get our answers."

Edison nodded. "I already started the return protocol. However, it will take a few minutes to reconfigure the program. It calls for *Journey II* to make several orbital rotations before the elevator brings it back."

He returned his attention to Hondo and Carly. Each floated weightless beside one another in the cargo bin. Faces fixed in blissful slumber, their fingers touched almost like they were holding hands. Edison couldn't take his eyes off them, and he fought to keep his mind—taunt with emotion—focused on their safe return.

"They're going to be okay, right?" Bree stood next to him, hands held to her mouth, eyes bright with shock.

Lost in the stunning discovery, Edison had forgotten all about her.

Although shaken at the sight of Hondo and Carly's sudden appearance on the module, Bree's close friendship with Carly must have made it even worse for her.

"I think so," he tried to assure her. Then, with more bravado than he felt, added, "The launch and return to earth shouldn't have any harmful effect on them."

A loud *ping* sounded, and the synthesized female voice announced, *"Initiating descent protocol."*

A pent up breath escaped from Edison at the announcement. *Finally, some good news.*

He turned from Bree, anxious to get started. But before he

could tap a key, the control panels all throughout the tower lit up like Christmas trees.

With red lights.

A klaxon blared, so loud Bree covered her ears, followed by the synthetic voice. It repeatedly boomed two words which drove a dagger of ice into Edison's heart.

System failure.

Edison felt like a roundhouse had been delivered straight into his stomach.

Frantically, he barked, "Enable systems diagnostic." As he scanned the data scrolling rapid-fire across the screen, the blood drained from his face.

"No," he whispered.

Stanton Jones rushed to his side. "What is it? What happened?"

"The program has been corrupted," Edison replied. "The coding is unspooling, and if we don't do something to stop it, *Journey II* will shut down along with the anti-gravity rings. The entire system is at risk!"

Jones took the news with a grim nod. "We'll worry about how this happened later. For now, what are our options?"

Edison's mind raced. Every possibility and avenue slammed into a brick wall. There *were* no options. Time was their biggest obstacle, and it would soon run out for his friends trapped inside the doomed module.

He reached a decision. "Shut down all systems!" he ordered. Seconds later, the anti-gravity rings began to drop one-by-one. Friction soon turned them into streaks of light and smoke as they entered the atmosphere. Onboard *Journey II*, the interior video went blank.

"Edison, what are you doing?" Jones cried.

Edison held up his hand to forestall any more questions. He started a silent countdown from ten.

Please God, please let this work.

At zero, he barked, "Reboot all onboard systems. Restrict only to life support and communications."

There was no way to know how widespread the corruption had traveled before he shut everything down. If the decay of the coding proceeded to include the module's systems, they could do nothing.

And his friends would die.

He held his breath. His eyes, along with dozens of others, remained glued to the monitor. Seconds dragged by. The silence within the control center was so complete, the *ping* echoed like a gunshot.

"System integrity restored," the synthetic voice announced.

The interior image of the module came to life, and a collective sigh of relief coursed through the control tower.

Edison swiveled to face his grandpa. "Somehow, malware was introduced into our launch and descent protocols. I had to shut everything down before the virus spread any further. I took an educated guess that it would start with the anti-gravity coils, then the anti-grav rings, and finish with the space module."

Edison raised a shaky hand to his face and rubbed his eyes. "In a hospital, sometimes doctors have to amputate an infected arm or leg to stop the spread of infection. I thought if I jettisoned part of the programming—separated it—it would isolate *Journey II* from the virus. That was all I could think of to do."

Stanton Jones gripped Edison's shoulder. "You made the right call. Your quick thinking saved the life of your friends.

Temperatures are at absolute zero in outer space. That's minus four hundred and fifty-nine degrees Fahrenheit, and without the module's life support system, Hondo and Carly would have frozen to death within a matter of minutes. You did the only thing you could do."

Edison shook his head. "All I did was buy some time, Grandpa. And I had to sacrifice the anti-gravity rings." He looked up.

"Now we have no way to bring Hondo and Carly back to earth."

CHAPTER 46

SILENCE GREETED EDISON'S ANNOUNCEMENT.

The doors of the elevator whisked open and Carney rushed into the control center. He froze at the sight of the ocean of somber faces. "What's going on?"

Stanton Jones gestured at one of the large monitors. Tight-lipped, he said, "We found Hondo and Carly. They're onboard *Journey*."

Carney gaped at the motionless pair drifting side-by-side.

"And it gets worse. Someone sabotaged the anti-gravity elevator by introducing a viral worm into the programming. It managed to infect much of the coding before Edison could shut it down."

"But how?" Carney asked. "We have a closed system and firewalls in place for these kinds of threats."

Jones' nostrils flared. "It could only have come from within. The saboteur must be one of us, a LogicTech employee with a high security clearance—one high enough to have password authorization."

"It doesn't matter!"

Startled, the two men looked over to see Edison point at the video feed of his friends. "Hondo and Carly are trapped on *Journey*! We must get them back or they will die!"

He turned the hoverchair and propelled it toward one of the large observation windows. The LogicTech scientists parted to let him pass, and Edison came to a stop at the window's edge. Below him the tarmac shimmered in the afternoon heat. He stared, the image wavering as his eyes filled with tears.

Bree followed Edison, and knelt beside him. "You'll think of something. You always do."

Edison struck the arm of the hoverchair chair with his fist. "You don't understand! Even if we remove the virus, the programming for the return of *Journey II* back to earth is still damaged beyond repair. Even *if* we could restore the coding, we have no anti-gravity rings. When I shut the system down, they were pulled back to earth. By now, reentry and friction with the atmosphere has turned them into a vapor cloud. Without them the elevator is useless—"

He turned away, unable to continue, and gazed at the vista before him. The launch aprons were laid out like crop circles in front of the control tower. Off to the side, almost like an afterthought, was a small pad of concrete.

The original launch site of *Journey I*.

At the sight, a glimmer of an idea floated into Edison's mind. Nebulous, the pieces of a plan—like bits of code—swirled about as he struggled to pull his thoughts into focus. Then in a flash, a solution presented itself.

He sat bolt upright.

Edison grabbed the tablet in his lap and began to run calculations, numbers racing by in a blur. A minute passed. Then another. No one spoke, as if all within the control tower held their collective breath at the sight of Edison's furious efforts.

A final set of numbers scrolled onto the tablet. Edison's eyes widened at the sight. He raised his fist into the air and cried, "Yes!"

With a crisp pivot, the anti-grav chair shot toward Stanton Jones. "Grandpa! I know how we can save them."

Breathless, he gushed, "We can use *Journey I* to get Hondo and Carly back!"

Edison's announcement was met with stunned silence.

Impatient, Edison continued, "We must hurry. At the current rate of depletion, the oxygen levels on the module will red-line in two hours. We need to roll out *Journey I* and prep it—"

"Wait!" Stanton Jones interjected. "Are you saying use the same test module that almost crashed? Are you serious?"

Edison crossed his arms. "Yes. And remember, it didn't crash. *Journey I* made a successful return back to earth." He tapped the tablet and a graphic complete with timeline appeared on the control room monitors.

"We launch the original test module, and use its anti-gravity elevator to place it next to *Journey II*. Both space pods have exterior hatches designed for docking. We dock the two spacecraft, retrieve Hondo and Carly, place them on *Journey I*, and bring her home."

Jones speared Edison with a hard look. "And who would pilot the test module?"

Edison placed the tablet flat on his lap and returned his grandfather's gaze. "Me."

Jones chopped his hand. "No. Absolutely not!"

"But, Grandpa, I'm the only one familiar enough with the systems."

"I said no. End of discussion!"

Edison felt his face turn red. "So we just let my friends die? When I can save them?"

Jones waved his arm. "We'll get someone else. I'm sure we can find a test pilot to take your place."

"Who? Where? This isn't a plane, it's a space module. I'm the only one who knows how to maneuver *Journey I*."

Stanton Jones' steely façade crumbled. His spine, normally ramrod straight, slumped. "I lost your mother and father," he said in a choked whisper. "You are all I have left. I can't lose you too."

Edison moved closer. He took his grandfather's hand in his own. "When you made the decision to send me to a public school, I didn't want to go. I was scared and thought kids would point at me like I was some kind of freak, someone to be pitied and not taken seriously. All I wanted was to be left alone and be by myself, just like always."

He squeezed Jones' hand. "But you were right, Grandpa. I made friends, and got involved in a bunch of different things." Edison looked over at Bree. "Now I can't imagine going back to the way things used to be."

Edison pointed upward. "Hondo and Carly are in that module, and they're part of my life—the one you helped me to choose. If I can save them, and you don't let me try, then how can I live with myself? I would have been better off staying holed up in the mansion. I mean, isn't friendship supposed to be more than just about ourselves?"

Jones nodded, a sad smile on his face. "It is indeed." He rubbed the sudden moisture that appeared in his eyes. "You're confident you can retrieve Hondo and Carly from *Journey II*?"

Edison nodded.

Jones squeezed Edison's shoulder. "Then go get your friends."

CHAPTER 47

THE NEXT HOUR FLEW BY IN A BLUR.

Journey I, taken out of storage, now sat perched on the small concrete apron, the hard tarmac dwarfed by the much larger launch sites. There had been little time to retrofit the test module and its anti-gravity elevator. However, workers had managed to secure cargo netting to *Journey I's* interior, and it would be used to strap in Hondo and Carly on the trip back to earth. The command chair, formerly held Bob the Mannequin's seat, was removed. Edison's hoverchair, itself an anti-gravity device, would be used instead. Removal of the heavy piece of equipment would compensate somewhat for the additional mass of Hondo and Carly.

The life support system aboard *Journey I*—never designed to support three people—could not be upgraded in time. Instead, Edison planned to wear an environmental suit he fashioned himself. Made of a heat and cold resistant polycarbonate fabric, the gray experimental suit was also airtight and carried its own oxygen supply. By his calculations, Edison determined this would leave sufficient oxygen for his friends to make the return trip to earth.

Because of the contamination of LogicTech's command computer, most of the launch and return of *Journey I* would be done the hard way.

By manual control.

A pair of control grips—similar to those found with video games—now perched securely on each arm of the anti-grav chair. Like throttles, they were key to the operation of the anti-gravity elevator, and Edison would use them to pilot the module. In addition, *Journey's* onboard computer was slaved to these controls. Great care was taken to sever any connection to LogicTech's mainframe, and therefore, prevent any possible corruption from the viral worm which infected *Journey II*. This trade-off also meant Edison would be further isolated, and could expect no help from LogicTech's considerable technical resources.

He would be on his own.

Every passing second left Edison more on edge, and he constantly checked the oxygen levels on *Journey II*. Anxious to get started, he waited impatiently on the sunbaked asphalt as his grandfather directed technicians to make yet another systems check on *Journey I*.

A trickle of sweat streaked down his neck. He pulled at the suit's fabric which adhered to his body like a second skin. Edison tugged on Stanton Jones sleeve. "Grandpa, our window of opportunity gets smaller every minute we spend here. It's time to launch."

Jones nodded. "I know. Putting off the inevitable, I suppose." He reached down and put his arms around Edison, lifting him halfway out of his seat with the fierceness of his hug. "No matter what happens, I want you to remember one thing."

"Sure, Grandpa. What is it?"

"I love you. I always have and I always will."

Eyes bright with tears, Jones released Edison and stepped back.

Carney moved forward and took Edison's hand in a firm handshake. "Good luck. Be careful and bring everyone back safe and sound. Including you!"

Emotions roiled inside Edison. He took a deep breath and was about to propel the hoverchair to the open hatch, when another pair of arms suddenly enveloped him. They were warm and soft, and a stray tendril of lavender-scented hair tickled his nose.

Bree.

"You're the bravest person I've ever met," she sniffled, tears streaking her cheeks. "I'm going to pray for you every second until you're back safely on the ground with Hondo and Carly." Bree leaned closer. "Don't take any foolish chances." She kissed his cheek and pivoted to join Jones and Carney.

Edison swallowed, a hard lump rising in his throat. He toggled the anti-grav chair's controls, and was soon aboard *Journey I*.

"Secure," he commanded. The electromagnets locked the hoverchair in place. Next he closed the outside hatch. With a *click*, it levered shut.

All external noise abruptly ended. The silence within the module was so complete, only the *shish, shish, shish* of the atmospheric recycling system could be heard.

Edison checked the chronometer on his wrist. Counting down, the digital display showed less than an hour and fifteen minutes. It would take thirty to forty-five minutes for the anti-gravity elevator to place *Journey I* in orbit next to its sister module. Another ten to fifteen to maneuver and dock the two space modules. By this time, Hondo and Carly would have, at best, only about twenty minutes of breathable air left. Edison would have to retrieve both of them and get them onboard *Journey I* within this short period of time.

Or they would suffocate.

Edison activated his visual controls. A pair of holographic displays appeared before him. On his left was the global positioning of both *Journey I* and *II*. Edison would use this holograph to guide him toward the sister module. Hovering directly in front of him was a ghostly image of *Journey I*. Like the scope on a gun, crosshairs were centered on the module, and indicated the list of the spacecraft. This delicate balance between the anti-gravity rings and the module's gyros—normally regulated by a computer—needed to work in concert. Otherwise, *Journey I* would drop out of the space elevator's influence, and fall back to earth.

And these were the same faulty gyros which almost caused a crash the first time.

Edison manipulated the control grips. A bubble—like that on a carpenter's level—appeared on the holographic crosshairs. The bubble represented *Journey's* pitch and parabolic path to orbit. Edison knew he had to try and keep it centered as much as possible.

He could delay no longer. Their window of time continued to shrink. He activated the anti-gravity coils.

With a slight *bump*, the space pod rose into the air.

CHAPTER 48

THE MODULE ROSE LESS THAN A HUNDRED FEET WHEN THE FIRST sign of trouble appeared.

The balky gyros caused an erratic yaw which Edison fought to control. The bubble on his display swung off-center again and again. Each time, his deft adjustments via the controller grips prevented disaster. The spacecraft continued to inch higher, the progress slow but steady.

The tense atmosphere slowed time almost to a standstill. When Edison risked a glance at his chronometer, it showed less than ten minutes had passed.

It felt like an hour.

Journey I's progress was too slow. It would not get him to the rendezvous with her sister module in time. Fresh despair gripped Edison. *Hondo and Carly are going to suffocate before I can get to them.*

"No! I can't think this way," he whispered. He grit his teeth. "I *will* save my friends!"

With renewed determination, he gripped the controllers and fought for the lives of his friends.

Journey I continued her trek upward through the atmosphere, Edison making constant adjustments. With each passing mile, Edison became more adept at guiding the module. His corrections became quicker, the pauses less frequent. Soon, the spacecraft rose without interruption. So fierce was Edison's concentration, he didn't realize they had reached geosynchronous orbit until a *ping* chimed to signal *Journey's* arrival.

Edison checked the chronometer. *Fifty-five minutes.* His window to retrieve Hondo and Carly had shrunk to only twenty-five minutes.

He pushed the lip mike up to his mouth. *"Journey I* in stable orbit."

"Roger that, *Journey*," Stanton Jones replied, the relief evident in his voice. "Do you see the package yet?"

Edison activated the radar array. A red, pulsing dot appeared on the holograph. As he watched, it moved closer and closer. "Affirmative. Anticipate rendezvous in ten to fifteen minutes."

"Good." After a pause, the LogicTech CEO's voice continued, "Godspeed, Grandson. Go get your friends."

Hearing his grandfather's voice warmed the ice in Edison's heart that had followed him all the way from the surface. A smile appeared on his lips. "I got this, Grandpa. *Journey* out."

Edison steeled himself for the next crucial stage.

First, he used the anti-gravity elevator to hold *Journey I* in place while *Journey II's* orbital motion brought the sister spacecraft to him. Then, he had to match her orbital speed. Next, he would use thrusters to maneuver close enough to dock both modules. The thrusters—nothing more than nozzles which released compressed gas—were embedded in the metallic exoskeleton and could swivel in any direction. In the weightlessness of space, this gave the module pinpoint maneuverability.

Powerful magnets ringed each spacecraft's docking sites. When activated, the modules would be held together in an airtight grip.

At least, that's how they are supposed to work, Edison thought. *They've never been tested before.*

He followed *Journey II's* progress on the radar. Closer and closer she drew until the module was within a quarter mile of *Journey I*. Edison manipulated the controllers and slowly brought the spacecraft nearer and nearer. When the two modules were within a hundred yards of one another, Edison switched on the exterior cameras. He spotted a glorious sight.

Journey II.

Now with a sightline, he activated the thrusters and began the dance to bring two multi-ton hunks of metal together with the softness of a butterfly's kiss.

Distance shrank from yards to feet, then from feet to inches. Three times, Edison attempted to dock, and three times, failed to do so. The last attempt resulted in a *screech* of metal skin as both modules scraped past one another.

Edison sharpened his determination. He edged *Journey I* closer for another attempt. *Journey II's* stubby docking port—like a fireplug—flared outward several feet. Inch by agonizing inch, he moved nearer. So close he could now see the airtight flange with the *LogicTech* logo stenciled on it, his fingers touched the controller and made a final adjustment.

With a gentle *bump*, the two spacecraft touched.

Edison activated the magnets. With a *shiver*, *Journey I* joined with its sister module. Edison hit the release on the safety harness and pushed himself up. Weightless, he floated like a feather. Just like swimming, he was in his element.

Legs weren't necessary in space.

Edison pulled himself along with handholds spaced at intervals within the module. When he reached the docking portal, a green light mounted next to it blinked on and off. He studied the readout on the small monitor next to the light, and nodded in satisfaction.

The magnetic seal was holding and showed no loss of atmospheric integrity.

With no time to lose, Edison touched a sensor embedded in his suit, and a helmet telescoped over his head. It joined the fabric at his neck with a *hiss*, to form an airtight seal. Canned air filled the helmet. It carried with it a stale, sterile odor, but Edison was taking no chances. The breathable air in *Journey II* was already at a critical stage. He needed to move fast.

Edison hit the master control, and the shroud sealing *Journey I's* dock slid open. The sister module's gray metal exoskeleton appeared, but rather than a green light, a red warning flash greeted him. He bit back a groan. *What now?*

A sealed control panel provided access to the docking mechanism. He struggled to shove it open, the cold metal plate resisting his attempts. Finally, he managed to pry a gap wide enough to activate the master control switch.

Nothing happened.

He tried again and again with no results. Frustrated, Edison sat back and tried to think. *There's no time for this. Why isn't it working?*

Then a possible reason for the problem came to him. The problem with *Journey I's* first test launch was a faulty gyro—caused by inadequate insulation of the wiring. With temperatures in outer space at absolute zero, maybe the same thing happened to the docking controls on *Journey II*. If so, what he needed to do was warm up the control panel and cabling to allow the electrical impulses to move.

But how?

He checked his chronometer. *Five minutes.* Only five minutes before the buildup of carbon dioxide suffocated his friends.

Think, Edison, think!

CHAPTER 49

A FIRM PUSH LAUNCHED EDISON BACK TO THE SMALLER SPACECRAFT. Like *Journey II*, this module contained cargo bins. He caught one of the handholds and steadied himself. With the other hand he hit the release lever on the nearest storage container. An outer panel *whished* open to reveal several bundles secured within small steel baskets.

Please, please let it be here, Edison prayed.

He reached into the nearest basket for a rectangular metal case the size and shape of a shoebox. He removed the Velcro straps holding the case, and it floated free. Edison grabbed it and released the catch to open the lid. At the sight of the object within, he breathed a sigh of relief.

Nestled within a cocoon of soft, foam rubber lay a portable plasma welder.

Although only a test module, part of *Journey I*'s design covered all contingencies. This included repairs. In orbit one couldn't call a mechanic or a technician to fix a problem, the most serious problem being atmospheric leaks. Among possible sources of these leaks were structural flaws and collisions with micro-meteors. Tools to fix onboard issues therefore became part of *Journey I*'s preparations prior to her launch. When the test module was put in storage, Edison had no way of knowing if these implements aboard had been removed.

The answer now lay in his hand.

He pushed away and pulled himself back to *Journey II's* docking controls. Self-igniting and with its own fuel source of argon and hydrogen gases, special care must be taken with the plasma welder. All he needed to do was to heat the metal and wiring inside enough to get electrical current moving again. The last thing he needed was molten drops of metal floating around. If one came in contact with his suit, it could burn a hole in it and cause the loss of his oxygen supply.

Then he would be in the same fix as his friends—struggling to breathe. Without him to pilot *Journey I* back to the surface, they would die.

With great care, he ignited the welder and ran the white-hot arc all along the metal plate securing the controls. He tried the master switch again.

Nothing.

He repeated the process, dragging the arc as long as he dared on the metal panel. Without warning, the red light flared to green.

Success!

An audible *whoosh* announced the retreat of the docking seal and the equalization of atmospheric pressure between the two modules.

A narrow tunnel mated the two spacecraft, and Edison launched himself through it. He shot into *Journey II's* control room and rebounded against the hard steel wall. He ignored the pain from the bruising impact and checked the data device on his wrist. The blood left his face in a rush at the breakdown of air within the module.

Oxygen 11.3%, Nitrogen 79.6%, Carbon dioxide 11.9%.

Earth's atmosphere—normally a mixture of 78% nitrogen, 20.9% oxygen, and 6.5% carbon dioxide—was the ideal combination of gases which both modules tried to maintain. Recycling filters aboard the spacecraft worked to removed excess gases, particularly carbon dioxide, and maintain this delicate blend of air. However, this balance had been upended on *Journey II*. Now the level of carbon dioxide exceeded that of oxygen.

Suffocation was imminent.

Edison hauled himself to the cargo bin where Hondo and Carly drifted like feathers, faces still fixed in a picture of serenity.

Except their lips were blue, and both hiccupped one gasp after another.

Edison released the straps on a small backpack he carried and pulled it in front of him. He reached inside and grabbed two cylinders with plastic masks and tubes. Used by paramedics and first responders, the cylinders were portable cannisters of oxygen. Hondo was nearest, so he slipped the mask over his friend's face first. With a twist of a knob, a *hiss* of oxygen filled the mask. With no time left to lose, he pulled Carly to him and repeated the process.

He studied his friends. "C'mon, c'mon," he pleaded.

He grabbed Hondo's wrist and felt for a pulse. Thready at first, it became stronger, the fish-out-of-water gasps less frequent. He quickly switched to Carly and found her pulse also more robust. The tinge of blue on their lips faded to a normal, pink-rose color.

Relief flooded Edison. *I got to them in time!*

The next step involved getting his friends aboard *Journey I*. Edison grabbed Hondo with one hand and pulled himself along with the other. He left him drifting by the umbilical connecting the two spacecraft, then went back and retrieved Carly. Like a caboose, he tugged her along through the narrow tunnel and into *Journey I*.

A gentle nudge sent them to the cargo netting where he

secured Carly. Edison wrapped her like a mummy, gave each strap a final tug, and nodded in satisfaction.

Then he retrieved Hondo.

Getting his large friend through the narrow umbilical proved to be a challenge. Hondo's torso, not much smaller than the passageway, filled every inch of it. Edison managed to arrange Hondo's arms straight up like someone diving into a pool. With his shoes dragging against the sides, he pulled his friend, foot-by-foot, through the tight confines.

At last, they exited into the smaller spacecraft. Edison fastened Hondo within the cargo netting, then removed the oxygen masks and stowed them and the cannisters into the backpack. Both his friends now breathed normally. With only the return trip left to the earth's surface, the oxygen level within the module should be sufficient for all of them.

Edison tapped the sensor on his suit and the helmet disappeared back into the polycarbonate fabric. A sigh of relief escaped his lips. After the sterile oxygen within his suit, *Journey I's* air was like a bouquet.

Sweat beaded his forehead, and he swiped at it with the back of his hand. Droplets floated away like beads on a necklace. He ignored them, propelled himself to his hoverchair, and strapped in.

Let's go home.

"Disengage."

A tremor shook *Journey I* at Edison's order. The airtight seal slid back in place and the docking magnets released their hold on the larger sister spacecraft. However, when Edison engaged the thrusters to pull away from *Journey II*, nothing happened. He increased the thrust and the smaller spacecraft shuddered. Edison quickly throttled back.

Huh? What happened?

"Run diagnostics on docking mechanism," he ordered. Seconds ticked by as the computer complied.

"Journey II not uncoupled," the computer's pleasant female voice announced.

"Why?"

Another few seconds passed. *"Journey II's docking magnets are still locked in place,"* the artificial voice replied.

Frustrated, Edison said, "Isolate problem with the magnets."

The answer took longer this time. *"Master control unresponsive."*

Edison's heart sank. The plasma welder must have damaged the internal wiring—even partially melted them—although there could be a hundred other reasons why.

"Solutions?"

This time the answer came instantly. *"Replace docking controls."*

Now they were in real trouble.

CHAPTER 50

EDISON SAT BACK AND CONSIDERED POSSIBLE SOLUTIONS.

The docking magnets on *Journey II* were powerful, and the chances the smaller spacecraft could break free were nonexistent. Even so he tried anyway, and used the thrusters to rock back and forth. All this act accomplished was to set off a blare of alarms along with an array of red warning lights.

Next he shut down *Journey II's* electrical grid completely in hopes of forcing the magnets to disengage. It had no effect. He tried one last Hail Mary, and rebooted the system. A faint chance existed the problem resulted from a computer glitch, and the restart might resolve the problem.

Nothing. The two spacecraft remained locked together.

Edison closed his eyes. A sense of hopelessness filled him. To have come this far, to have rescued his friends, and to be so close to a safe return—only to have a faulty electrical system stop them dead in their tracks.

"No!" he shouted, his voice an angry echo which resounded within the module. "There must be a solution, and I'm going to find it!"

He pressed knuckles into his eyes and leaned forward, his mind working furiously. Neurons flared, synapses fired, and his thoughts flashed by at astonishing speed. Edison's mind shuffled possible remedies like cards, his discard pile growing with each passing second.

Then he drew an ace.

Edison sat up, his eyes wide. "There's no way *Journey I* can detach from the docking magnets," he whispered. "Her mass is too small."

Triumphant, he sat higher. "But *Journey II* can!"

Holographic numerals floated wraithlike before Edison's eyes. Aided by the onboard computer, he crunched the numbers at a dizzying pace. He ran the calculations again and again until he was convinced they were correct. A wide grin crossed his face.

I found a way.

The euphoria left him in a rush when he considered how small their margin of error would be, and the reaction of his grandpa when he explained what he intended to do.

Edison keyed the lip mike. "*Journey I* to LogicTech control. Hondo and Carly have been recovered. They were extracted in time, repeat extracted in time."

Stanton Jones' voice crackled to life. "Wonderful news!" In the background cheers rang out at the announcement. After a pause the LogicTech CEO continued, "What is your ETA?"

Edison swallowed. "Uh, that depends. We have a problem." Quickly, he explained the malfunction of the docking controls and the inability to separate from the larger spacecraft.

"What do you propose?" His grandfather's question carried with it an edge of wariness.

Edison steeled himself. "I'm going to descend rapidly. At forty miles—about halfway through the mesosphere—I'll use the anti-gravity elevator to stop *Journey I*'s descent. At that distance, gravity's pull should be sufficient to separate *Journey II*'s larger mass from *Journey I*. It will snap off like a dry twig."

At least according to the computer-generated scenarios.

Jones didn't answer. The pause dragged so long, Edison thought the communication link had failed.

Finally, his grandfather's voice reappeared. "That seems high risk. What happens if this separation fails?"

Edison now took his time to reply. He sighed and with a shake of his head said, "Then both modules fall out of control and burn up in the earth's atmosphere."

A sharp intake of breath greeted his pronouncement. "I see. I'd ask if you have explored other options, but I already know the answer." His grandpa's voice cracked, and Edison could tell he struggled to keep speaking.

"What do you need from us?"

Edison replied, "The design of the anti-gravity rings are for gradual ascents and descents. I'll have to reconfigure the space elevator because I'll be coming in hot, very hot. Friction with the atmosphere will produce heat barely within the tolerance specs. We'll need fire control teams on the tarmac to douse the module and cool it off quickly. Medical teams need to be there for obvious reasons, especially for Hondo and Carly. They seem okay, but I don't know how long they were in a low-oxygen environment. They'll each require complete physical examinations."

"Okay. Anything else?"

Edison managed a weak smile. "Well, Bree said she would pray for us. Maybe a few more prayers wouldn't hurt, huh, Grandpa?"

After a pause, Jones replied, "No. No it wouldn't hurt at all." The LogicTech CEO added, "Get home safe. Just get home safe."

"I will, Grandpa. I'm going to start our descent. I'll link the onboard computer with the control tower so you can keep track of our progress for as long as possible.

Journey I out."

Edison sent up his own silent prayer for himself and his friends, then prepared for what would undoubtedly be the wildest ride of his life.

He pulled his hoverchair harness tighter, made sure the electromagnets were at full power and locked in place, then gripped each controller firmly.

Let's do this.

"Initiate," he commanded.

A slight tremor shook the module, the only evidence their descent had begun. Eyes glued to the holographic image of the side-by-side spacecraft, Edison watched the pitch, *Journey I*'s gyros already engaged to keep the sister modules steady. As they drew closer and earth's gravity became stronger, the struggle to keep their list under control and aligned with the anti-gravity rings would be increasingly difficult.

Gradual at first, the downward trajectory accelerated. Like on a carnival ride, Edison felt his stomach inch toward his throat. This acceleration—critical to free *Journey I* from *Journey II*—would continue until they reached the necessary speed to carry out the maneuver during their plunge through the mesosphere.

The desperate gambit, fraught with danger, could end only one of two ways. Either the larger spacecraft's momentum and greater mass would cause it to snap off, or the two modules would stay joined and become fireballs plunging to earth.

A digital countdown joined the holograph. Edison spared it

a quick glance, his hands full keeping the spacecraft from toppling over. Closer and closer the target altitude came. The entire module shook, a low rumble rising to a roar in intensity. The heat within the module rose as well, and rivulets of sweat poured down Edison's face.

Journey I dropped faster and faster, the countdown now down to single seconds. The module shook like a giant's hand had closed around it in a game of catch. A *ping, ping, ping* knifed through the roar.

Then they reached the target altitude.

"All stop!" Edison cried.

The sudden deceleration jerked the module back and forth, and only the safety harness kept Edison from being catapulted from his seat. He fought to keep the spacecraft stable, but despite his best efforts, *Journey I* began a slow but relentless drift. She was only moments away from tumbling out of the space elevator and to their fiery deaths. Edison didn't need to glance at the holographic images to know the reason.

They had failed to break free of *Journey II*.

CHAPTER 51

"Position all thrusters toward *Journey II*!" Edison cried. Immediately the blast jets swiveled toward the sister spacecraft.

"Full thrust!" *Journey I*'s tilt slowed a fraction as the smaller module attempted to push away.

In the weightlessness of outer space, the compressed gas thrusters were an effective means of propulsion even with an object the size and tonnage of *Journey I*. Once in the grip of earth's gravity, however, Edison's ability to move the heavy spacecraft by such means was slight at best. The nudge—feeble though it might be—was the best he could do.

Such a slender thread to hold the balance of their lives on but Edison was out of options.

The bubble in the holographic display drifted to the edge of the crosshairs. The module's tilt became so pronounced, Edison slid sideways in the hoverchair despite the safety harness.

Crack.

A shudder shook the module, and like a cork, the spacecraft bobbed wildly in the opposite direction. Only Edison's quick adjustment of the gyros saved this sudden fluctuation from bouncing *Journey I* out of the anti-gravity stream. He immediately shut down the thrusters and activated the outside cameras—just in time to see the tumbling image of *Journey II* disappear from sight.

I did it! We broke free!

His elation quickly evaporated at the realization the most difficult stage still lay ahead.

A safe landing.

The normal descent and landing protocol was jettisoned in the desperate maneuver to shake free of *Journey II*. The tactic was an all-in proposition with no going back, and no time to recalibrate the anti-gravity rings. Not while falling like a brick. Even now the module's acceleration had resumed. A glance at the holographic readout showed *Journey I* rapidly approaching terminal velocity, fifty-three meters per second.

Edison's plan—to continue in freefall—allowed only for adjustments to keep *Journey I* within the confluence of the anti-gravity elevator, slowing the spacecraft just enough to prevent friction from melting its outer shell. This would all change, however, once they arrived a quarter mile above the earth's surface.

Then the real action would start.

The anti-gravity rings would be stacked like donuts below *Journey I*, then he would initiate her brutal deceleration. The method would stretch the limits of the module's structural integrity as each anti-gravity ring would be sacrificed to slow down the spacecraft. This would be no delicate or fine-tuned act, but a raw application of physics—force equals mass times acceleration, or in this case, *deceleration*.

Each anti-gravity ring would employ full power to push against the module and slow her down. A single anti-grav disk could not stop the speed or acceleration of a heavy mass like *Journey I*. The module would overwhelm the anti-gravity ring's ability to brake her freefall, and like an overinflated tire, the anti-grav device would blow out.

Then the next ring in line would do the same, flame out, and the next and the next, until each anti-gravity device had been used and destroyed. This collective effort of each sacrificed anti-gravity device would create a waterfall effect. *Journey I* would be pushed against, then fall, pushed again, fall again, but with each successive attempt, the descent would become shorter, the module's speed, reduced. By the time the spacecraft neared the launch apron, her velocity should be reduced to the point the combined efforts of the anti-gravity coils within *Journey I* and the launch apron could land her safely.

At least in theory.

Since nothing so far had worked out like the simulations, Edison prepared for everything. With this last step to land the module, however, there was little he could do one way or the other.

It would either work. Or not.

The heat within the module continued to rise the closer *Journey I* approached the quarter mile objective. Edison's skintight environmental suit made it feel like he was being boiled alive in his own sweat. Black spots swam before his eyes, and he fought to stay conscious. Ears dulled by the pounding of blood in his head, he heard the computer-generated voice start the countdown.

Breathing became a torturous exercise. Each breath of the hot air within the spacecraft seared his lungs like a blowtorch. The black spots, now the size of craters, dimmed his vision. *Got to hold on for a few more...*Edison's eyes closed and his chin dropped to his chest.

He passed into unconsciousness.

EDISON JONES AND THE ANTI-GRAV ELEVATOR

Ping, ping, ping.

The persistent sound roused Edison. He blinked and took a shaky breath of air so hot it felt like it blew straight out of a rotisserie. But he sensed something else as well. Their descent was slowing.

He *yelped* when this brief interlude ended with the space module dropping like a stone. Through hot, bleary eyes he studied the holographic readout and image.

They had reached the target altitude, the brief slowdown due to the effort of the first anti-gravity ring. More important, *Journey I* remained within the confluence of the space elevator. The landing strategy appeared to be working!

Edison's instinctively reached for the controller grips, then stopped. He could do nothing more now than hang on for the ride.

And what a ride it proved to be.

Sudden braking, followed by a drop similar to a trapdoor opening beneath the module. When Edison's spine wasn't grinding into the seat of the hoverchair, his stomach was trying to exit through his throat. The experience seemed to drag on for hours, but Edison's chronometer registered fewer than ten minutes passed.

Edison turned on the exterior cameras. The ground rushed toward them, the tiny images of the LogicTech Control Tower and launch aprons dotting the surface. More stop and go gripped the module as the spacecraft's descent continued to slow. Seconds later, the last anti-gravity ring fell away.

Only the anti-gravity coils were left.

The hard tarmac approached at a dizzying speed. Edison couldn't look.

He closed his eyes, unwilling to witness the crushing impact.

Suddenly, their downward motion halted. Edison cracked

an eyelid. Instead of the inevitable crash he expected, *Journey I* drifted earthward like a mote of dust. The spacecraft floated onto the hard concrete with a gentle thud. If not for his parched, raw throat, Edison would have shouted in triumph. *We did it!*

They made it home.

CHAPTER 52

The observation port revealed a phalanx of emergency vehicles converging on the spacecraft.

They slewed to a stop beside the grounded module. Fire hoses spun on reels as fire control personnel leaped into action. Water spewed from nozzles and cascaded on *Journey I*. Huge clouds of steam rose from the superheated metal. A *hiss*, like sizzling bacon, accompanied the action, and rose in pitch as more streams of water were added.

Edison released his safety harness and unlocked the hover chair's electromagnets. He spun the chair toward his friends who hung like limp dishtowels in the cargo netting.

Carly's face was cherry red, her skin slick with perspiration. Hondo dribbled sweat in such large quantities, a puddle formed on the space pod's floor.

Edison dug into his backpack and pulled out a biometric reader the size and shape of a bracelet. He slipped it on Carly's wrist, and when he tapped the small data device, her vitals appeared. After a few seconds of studying the readout, he sighed in relief.

Normal.

He quickly repeated the procedure with Hondo, and received the same positive results. His attention then turned to the efforts of the emergency personnel still dousing the module. The billows of steam were reduced to a thin vapor, and Edison judged it safe enough to open *Journey I*'s main hatch.

With a metallic *snick*, the door levered open, then descended to form a ramp. Cool November air poured into the compartment. Compared to the hot, stuffy air within *Journey I*, it felt like an arctic blast. Seconds later, Stanton Jones charged into the spacecraft, medical personnel pushing gurneys close on his heels. His grandfather raced to Edison's side.

"Are you okay?" Jones demanded. Without waiting for an answer, he ran his hands up and down Edison in a search of contusions and broken bones.

"Grandpa, I'm—"

Edison never got a chance to finish before he found himself wrapped him in a rib-crushing embrace. "Thank God you're okay." Tears of relief filled Jones' eyes.

The LogicTech CEO cleared his throat. "How are your friends?"

"I checked their biometrics, and they read normal," Edison croaked. "Do you have any water?" Jones produced a chilled bottle of water. Edison spun off the cap and greedily drank half the bottle, then wiped his mouth with his sleeve.

His throat, though still raw, felt much better. Edison pointed at Hondo and Carly being strapped onto the gurneys by paramedics. "Where are they taking them?"

"To our medical facility belowground. Once we've determined their condition, they will be transferred to the local hospital."

"Can I go with them?" Edison asked.

"You bet you are, especially since you'll join them for a full medical examination."

"But I feel just fine!" Edison protested.

Jones held up his hand. "No arguments. The only question is

how you'll get there. Either in your anti-grav chair, or on a gurney like your friends."

Edison knew better than to continue to protest, and followed the paramedics down the ramp. He blinked in the late afternoon light and paused at an unexpected sound.

Cheering.

He looked around. All the emergency personnel were clapping and shouting. It took him a second before he realized why.

It's for me. The applause is for me.

Although sore, tired, and bedraggled, he couldn't help the grin formed by his parched and cracked lips. It stayed with him all the way to the ambulance.

Inside the cramped vehicle, Edison wedged his hoverchair between Carly and Hondo. A saline drip swung from a harness above his friends, the plastic tubing threaded to a bag and attached to their motionless forms. Worry gnawed at Edison as the ambulance, lights flashing and siren blaring, sped away. The biometric scan he ran revealed only cursory information. There could still be more serious injuries.

A groan from Hondo interrupted his thoughts. His large friend blinked and let loose a jaw-cracking yawn.

Hondo looked around, and his eyes settled on Edison. "Man, I had the wildest dream." He smacked his lips. "You got anything to eat?"

Cutter Gentry's foot jammed the accelerator of the LogicTech cart to full power. He needed to get to the rendezvous as soon as possible. He figured he had an hour, maybe two before the manhunt began.

By then he needed to be out of the country.

He slammed his fist repeatedly onto the steering wheel. The action almost caused him to lose control of the speeding cart as it swerved off the road. He managed to regain command and veer back onto the asphalt, narrowly missing a stand of trees.

Damn that Jones boy!

The plan was perfect. The nosy brats on *Journey II* would die, LogicTech would be blamed, endless lawsuits would follow, and their efforts at spaceflight stopped in its tracks. NASA would never sanction another space launch by LogicTech. In the tech company's absence, Breakstone Industries would become the leader in launch technology. For his efforts, Gentry would become a wealthy man.

A *very* wealthy man.

When Jones allowed his crip grandson to attempt a rescue, Gentry could hardly contain his glee. The desperate act could only end in failure, plus the odds were good the snot-nosed kid would die in the attempt along with his friends. Manfred Breakstone would be ecstatic over this unexpected bonus—which had dollar signs written all over it.

Then his happy fantasy, complete with sipping frozen margaritas on a Bermuda beach—fat bank account in hand—evaporated. The impossible happened.

The Jones boy succeeded.

Gentry had watched the drama play out, at first with delight, then with growing trepidation. Every time it looked like the Jones brat faced certain death, he pulled a technological miracle out of his hat. In a million years, Gentry never would have believed the kid could pull it off until he witnessed it with his own eyes.

When *Journey I* safely touched down, he slipped out while everyone scrambled to meet the space pod.

The strip of pavement rounded a corner, and Gentry spotted

a LogicTech vehicle partially hidden within a copse of pine trees. Safely tucked away from the numerous security cameras covering every square inch of the giant underground facility, the rendezvous site ensured no unwanted surveillance. He pulled up next to the car and stopped. The same guard who helped him plant the virus in the LogicTech mainframe, got out and walked up over.

"Look, I've got to have an exit strategy," Gentry babbled. "I need Breakstone to—"

He stopped at the sight of the muzzle pointed at him, the blue-black gunmetal glinting in the light.

"What's this?" Gentry asked, eyes wide.

"You've become a loose end," the security guard replied. "And Mr. Breakstone doesn't like loose ends."

"I won't talk, I swear," Gentry pleaded.

The guard didn't answer. Instead he handed a folded piece of paper to Gentry. "Put this in your pocket. Now!" He gestured with the gun, and Gentry hastily stuffed it in his suit jacket.

"What is it?" he managed to ask.

A cruel smile appeared on the security guard's face. "A numbered account in the Caymans. It will take the feds some time to track down the origin of the funds, but once they do, it will lead to a Russian slush fund."

"Russians?"

The guard's smile grew wider. "Of course. Don't you watch the news? The Russkis are responsible for everything."

With a deft move, the counterfeit security guard drew another weapon from his pocket. He pointed the slim tapered end at Gentry. *Pfft*. A tiny blue dart sprouted from the NASA official's chest.

Gentry stiffened. He tried to pluck the barb from his chest, but his arms already felt like leaden weights.

The guard leaned closer. "One tranquillizer dart simply leaves you unconscious, while two," *pfft*, another dart appeared next to the first, "will leave you in a coma-like state. Three," *pfft*, a third dart joined the previous two, "stops your heart. Everyone will assume you committed suicide, and our loose end is eliminated neat and clean."

Gentry had difficulty hearing, as if the words came from a great distance. Head slumping forward, his chest rose and fell once, twice, then stilled.

The bogus security guard placed the tranquillizer gun in Gentry's hand, and closed his fingers firmly around it. He slipped off his latex gloves, stuffed them in his pocket, then got into his car.

He drove off without looking back.

CHAPTER 53

(Six months later)

THE END OF SCHOOL PARTY WAS IN FULL SWING.

Twenty of Edison's classmates frolicked in the water near the beach. The private lake stretched over two hundred acres, and had a dive platform floating about one hundred feet from the shore.

Music blared from a cabana adjacent to a large cabin. Carney flipped hamburgers and hotdogs over a grill, while chilled soft drinks floated like miniature icebergs in an old-fashioned wash basin. A pier and boat dock extended into the water from the cabana, and a pair of jet skis bobbed in the waves.

Edison declined another hot dog from Carney, then shook his head at the sight of Hondo demolishing his *fourth* hamburger. "Where do you put it?" he asked.

The last of the burger disappeared, and Hondo released a contented sigh. "I'm a growing boy," he pronounced. "Ask anybody."

In fact, Hondo had grown. It looked to Edison like his friend had shot up a foot since the incident with *Journey II*. The rest of Edison's first year in public school seemed to fly by. Besides the tests and homework, there were dances, basketball games, movies, and parties, each cherished memory a priceless treasure. His circle of friends continued to grow, but best of all, the part of him which felt so hollow and incomplete since the death of his parents, now seemed less empty.

His one regret was the inability to tie Breakstone Industries with the near disaster involving *Journey II*. Discovery of Cutter Gentry's body triggered an exhaustive investigation, yet no direct proof could be found tying the NASA official to Breakstone and the sabotage of his anti-grav elevator—although Edison's grandfather, Carney, and everyone else believed the rival technology company to be responsible.

Regardless, LogicTech's patent application for Edison's anti-gravity elevator was approved. More importantly, this came with NASA's endorsement. No more bureaucratic red tape for future launches.

All in all, the past nine months represented the happiest, most exciting time in Edison's life.

I wouldn't trade them for anything.

Edison gestured to Hondo. "Are you finished eating? I've got something I want to show you."

Hondo scratched his chin. "I think I'm good for now." He looked back at Carney. "Is the grill going to be open later?"

The burly bodyguard chuckled and waved them on. "Don't worry. I'll save half a dozen burgers for you."

Edison laughed at the look of relief on his friend's face. "Let's go."

Just then, Carly and Bree ran up to them. Carly wore a yellow bikini, and Bree wore a blue one piece bathing suit. Both girls dripped water, strands of wet hair like ropes plastered to their heads and necks.

"Where are you two going?" Carly asked.

Edison grinned. "You're just in time. I modified some jet skis with my anti-gravity device, and I'm going to get Hondo to help me try them out. Do you want to come along?"

In answer, both girls ran to the water's edge and jumped in. Hondo quickly overtook them as they swam to the bobbing jet skis. Edison beat them all when his hoverchair raced ahead on top of the water. Stopping beside the watercraft, Edison pushed himself out and splashed into the lake. He hoisted himself out of the water, into the seat, and then grabbed the jet ski's handles. Moments later, Hondo did the same on the other water craft.

Bree climbed aboard and sat behind Edison. She put her arms around him and held him tight. Carly joined Hondo on his jet ski and looped her arms around his waist.

Hondo looked over at Edison. "How do they work?"

Edison pointed at the throttle on the handle. "Same as an ordinary jet ski. You twist the throttle for more power or reverse to slow down."

Hondo nodded then turned to Edison. "Okay, I gotta ask. Why the modifications?"

Edison stared out at the water. When he replied, his voice had a bold edge to it. "Because there is a big solar system, a bigger galaxy, and an infinite universe out there. We've barely scratched the surface, and now we have the means to launch payloads into space, regardless of size and mass. The next step is to exploration, which means a brand new propulsion system will need to be invented."

Hondo eyed Edison. "And I suppose you already have one made up and ready to go in the bat cave you call your lab."

Edison glanced at his big friend, a grin on his face. "No, but I have a few ideas." He pointed ahead. "One loop around the lake. First one back to the dock wins."

With a *vroom,* the jet skis bounced out of the water and skimmed across the surface, the friends whooping in delight.

The start of what promised to be an endless summer.

On the tablet in her brother's hand, Hillary watched the jet skis race across the water.

Heller tapped the touchscreen and the saucer-shaped spy-drone rose higher and higher until the lake was no larger than a coin. Moments later, the drone zipped away and the image winked out.

The twins were in the same aircraft hangar the battle 'bots had fought in. Deserted, no one observed their eavesdropping.

Hillary looked at her brother, his evil smile a match for her own.

"When one can't beat one's opponent—" Hillary began.

"One steals from one's opponent," Heller finished.

The pair pivoted crisply and walked out.

ACKNOWLEDGEMENT

Many thanks to my fantastic critique group and countless author friends, fellow writers, and beta readers. Without their help, I'd struggle to complete a single sentence.

ABOUT THE AUTHOR

Michael Scott Clifton, a public educator for over 38 years as a teacher, coach, and administrator, currently lives in Mount Pleasant, Texas with his wife, Melanie and family cat. An avid gardener, reader, and movie junkie, he enjoys all kinds of book and movie genres. His books contain aspects of all the genres he enjoys—action, adventure, magic, fantasy, and romance. His fantasy novels, *The Janus Witch* and *The Open Portal* received 5-Star reviews from the prestigious Readers' Favorite Book Reviews, with The Janus Witch a regional selection by The Indie Author Project. A finalist in a number of short story contests, Edges of Gray won First Place in the Texas Authors Contest. Professional credits include articles published in the Texas Study of Secondary Education Magazine. Clifton's latest book, *The Open Portal,* launches the fantasy book series, *Conquest of the Veil*, with Book II, *Escape From Wheel*, to be released in 2020. Michael can be reached at msclifton955@gmail.com. Follow him at www.michaelscottclifton.com and at www.facebook.com/authormsclifton.

Made in the USA
Middletown, DE
17 September 2022